Texas Rangers 2020

A Baseball Companion

Edited by R.J. Anderson, Craig Goldstein and Bret Sayre

Baseball Prospectus

Craig Brown, Steven Goldman and David Pease, Consultant Editors
Robert Au, Harry Pavlidis and Amy Pircher, Statistics Editors

Copyright © 2020 by DIY Baseball, LLC.
All rights reserved

This book or any part thereof may not be reproduced or transmitted in any form or by any means, electronic or mechanical, including photocopying, recording, or by any information storage and retrieval system, without permission in writing from the publisher.

Limit of Liability/Disclaimer of Warranty: While the publisher and the author have used their best efforts in preparing this book, they make no representations or warranties with respect to the accuracy or completeness of the contents of this book and specifically disclaim any implied warranties of merchantability or fitness for a particular purpose. No warranty may be created or extended by sales representatives or written sales materials. The advice and strategies contained herein may not be suitable for your situation. You should consult with a professional where appropriate. Neither the publisher nor the author shall be liable for any loss of profit or any other commercial damages, including but not limited to special, incidental, consequential, or other damages.

Library of Congress Cataloging-in-Publication Data:
paperback
ISBN-13: 978-1-949332-90-2

Project Credits
Cover Design: Michael Byzewski at Aesthetic Apparatus
Interior Design and Production: Jeff Pease, Dave Pease
Layout: Jeff Pease, Dave Pease

Baseball icon courtesy of Uberux, from https://www.shareicon.net/author/uberux

Ballpark diagram courtesy of Lou Spirito/THIRTY81 Project, https://thirty81project.com/

Manufactured in the United States of America
10 9 8 7 6 5 4 3 2 1

Table of Contents

Statistical Introduction v

Part 1: Team Analysis

Texas Rangers: Where Are You Going, Where Have You Been? 3
  Ben Carsley, Samuel Hale and Matthew Trueblood
Performance Graphs 7
2019 Team Performance 8
2020 Team Projections 9
Team Personnel 10
Globe Life Park in Arlington Stats 11
Rangers Team Analysis 13

Part 2: Player Analysis

Rangers Player Analysis 20
Rangers Prospects 117

Part 3: Featured Articles

The Baseball Is Juiced (Again) 135
  Robert Arthur
The Moral Hazard of Playing It Safe 139
  Craig Goldstein

Index of Names 145

Statistical Introduction

Sports are, fundamentally, a blend of athletic endeavor and storytelling. Baseball, like any other sport, tells its stories in so many ways: in the arc of a game from the stands or a season from the box scores, in photos, or even in numbers. At Baseball Prospectus, we understand that statistics don't replace observation or any of baseball's stories, but complement everything else that makes the game so much fun.

What stats help us with is with patterns and precision, variance and value. This book can help you learn things you may not see from watching a game or hundred, whether it's the path of a career over time or the breadth of the entire MLB. We'd also never ask you to choose between our numbers and the experience of viewing a game from the cheap seats or the comfort of your home; our publication combines running the numbers with observations and wisdom from some of the brightest minds we can find. But if you *do* want to learn more about the numbers beyond what's on the backs of player jerseys, let us help explain.

Offense

We've revised our methodology for determining batting value. Long-time readers of the book will notice that we've retired True Average in favor of a new metric: Deserved Runs Created Plus (DRC+). Developed by Jonathan Judge and our stats team, this statistic measures everything a player does at the plate–reaching base, hitting for power, making outs, and moving runners over–and puts it on a scale where 100 equals league-average performance. A DRC+ of 150 is terrific, a DRC+ of 100 is average and a DRC+ of 75 means you better be an excellent defender.

DRC+ also does a better job than any of our previous metrics in taking contextual factors into account. The model adjusts for how the park affects performance, but also for things like the talent of the opposing pitcher, value of different types of batted-ball events, league, temperature and other factors. It's able to describe a player's expected offensive contribution than any other statistic we've found over the years, and also does a better job of predicting future performance as well.

There's a lot more to DRC+'s story, and you can read all about it in greater depth near the end of this book.

The other aspect of run-scoring is baserunning, which we quantify using Baserunning Runs. BRR not only records the value of stolen bases (or getting caught in the act), but also accounts for all the stuff that doesn't show up on the back of a baseball card: a runner's ability to go first to third on a single, or advance on a fly ball.

Defense

Where offensive value is *relatively* easy to identify and understand, defensive value is...not. Over the past dozen years, the sabermetric community has focused mostly on stats based on zone data: a real-live human person records the type of batted ball and estimated landing location, and models are created that give expected outs. From there, you can compare fielders' actual outs to those expected ones. Simple, right?

Unfortunately, zone data has two major issues. First, zone data is recorded by commercial data providers who keep the raw data private unless you pay for it. (All the statistics we build in this book and on our website use public data as inputs.) That hurts our ability to test assumptions or duplicate results. Second, over the years it has become apparent that there's quite a bit of "noise" in zone-based fielding analysis. Sometimes the conclusions drawn from zone data don't hold up to scrutiny, and sometimes the different data provided by different providers don't look anything alike, giving wildly different results. Sometimes the hard-working professional stringers or scorers might unknowingly inflict unconscious bias into the mix: for example good fielders will often be credited with more expected outs despite the data, and ballparks with high press boxes tend to score more line drives than ones with a lower press box.

Enter our Fielding Runs Above Average (FRAA). For most positions, FRAA is built from play-by-play data, which allows us to avoid the subjectivity found in many other fielding metrics. The idea is this: count how many fielding plays are made by a given player and compare that to expected plays for an average fielder at their position (based on pitcher ground ball tendencies and batter handedness). Then we adjust for park and base-out situations.

When it comes to catchers, our methodology is a little different thanks to the laundry list of responsibilities they're tasked with beyond just, well, catching and throwing the ball. By now you've probably heard about "framing" or the art of making umpires more likely to call balls outside the strike zone for strikes. To put this into one tidy number, we incorporate pitch tracking data (for the years it exists) and adjust for important factors like pitcher, umpire, batter and home-field advantage using a mixed-model approach. This grants us a number for how many strikes the catcher is personally adding to (or subtracting from) his pitchers' performance...which we then convert to runs added or lost using linear weights.

Framing is one of the biggest parts of determining catcher value, but we also take into account blocking balls from going past, whether a scorer deems it a passed ball or a wild pitch. We use a similar approach—one that really benefits from the pitch tracking data that tells us what ends up in the dirt and what doesn't. We also include a catcher's ability to prevent stolen bases and how well they field balls in play, and *finally* we come up with our FRAA for catchers.

Pitching

Both pitching and fielding make up the half of baseball that isn't run scoring: run prevention. Separating pitching from fielding is a tough task, and most recent pitching analysis has branched off from Voros McCracken's famous (and controversial) statement, "There is little if any difference among major-league pitchers in their ability to prevent hits on balls hit in the field of play." The research of the analytic community has validated this to some extent, and there are a host of "defense-independent" pitching measures that have been developed to try and extract the effect of the defense behind a hurler from the pitcher's work.

Our solution to this quandary is Deserved Run Average (DRA), our core pitching metric. DRA looks like earned run average (ERA), the tried-and-true pitching stat you've seen on every baseball broadcast or box score from the past century, but it's very different. To start, DRA takes an event-by-event look at what the pitchers does, and adjusts the value of that event based on different environmental factors like park, batter, catcher, umpire, base-out situation, run differential, inning, defense, home field advantage, pitcher role and temperature. That mixed model gives us a pitcher's expected contribution, similar to what we do for our DRC+ model for hitters and FRAA model for catchers. (Oh, and we also consider the pitcher's effect on basestealing and on balls getting past the catcher.)

It's important to note that DRA is set to the scale of runs allowed per nine innings (RA9) instead of ERA, which makes DRA's scale slightly higher than ERA's. The reason for this is because ERA tends to overrate three types of pitchers:

1. Pitchers who play in parks where scorers hand out more errors. Official scorers differ significantly in the frequency at which they assign errors to fielders.
2. Ground-ball pitchers, because a substantial proportion of errors occur on groundballs.
3. Pitchers who aren't very good. Better pitchers often allow fewer unearned runs than bad pitchers, because good pitchers tend to find ways to get out of jams.

Since the last time you picked up an edition of this book, we've also made a few minor changes to DRA to make it better. Recent research into "tunneling"—the act of throwing consecutive pitches that appear similar from a batter's point of view until after the swing decision point–data has given us a new contextual factor to account for in DRA: plate distance. This refers to the distance between successive pitches as they approach the plate, and while it has a smaller effect than factors like velocity or whiff rate, it still can help explain pitcher strikeout rate in our model.

New Pitching Metrics for 2020

We're including a few "new" pitching metrics in the book for the 2020 edition, though unlike last year, these numbers may be a little bit more familiar to those of you who have spent some time investigating baseball statistics.

Fastball Percentage

Our fastball percentage (FB%) statistic measures how frequently a pitcher throws a pitch classified as a "fastball," measured as a percentage of overall pitches thrown. We qualify three types of fastballs:

1. The traditional four-seam fastball;
2. The two-seam fastball or sinker;
3. "Hard cutters," which are pitches that have the movement profile of a cut fastball and are used as the pitcher's primary offering or in place of a more traditional fastball.

For example, a pitcher with a FB% of 67 throws any combination of these three pitches about two-thirds of the time.

Whiff Rate

Everybody loves a swing and a miss, and whiff rate (WHF) measures how frequently pitchers induce a swinging strike. To calculate WHF, we add up all the pitches thrown that ended with a swinging strike, then divide that number by a pitcher's total pitches thrown. Most often, high whiff rates correlate with high strikeout rates (and overall effective pitcher performance).

Called Strike Probability

Called Strike Probability (CSP) is a number that represents the likelihood that all of a pitcher's pitches will be called a strike while controlling for location, pitcher and batter handedness, umpire and count. Here's how it works: on each pitch, our model determines how many times (out of 100) that a similar pitch was called for a strike given those factors mentioned above, and when normalized for each batter's strike zone. Then we average the CSP for all pitches thrown by a pitcher in a season, and that gives us the yearly CSP percentage you see in the stats boxes.

As you might imagine, pitchers with a higher CSP are more likely to work in the zone, where pitchers with a lower CSP are likely locating their pitches outside the normal strike zone, for better or for worse.

Projections

Many of you aren't turning to this book just for a look at what a player has done, but for a look at what a player is going to do: the PECOTA projections. PECOTA, initially developed by Nate Silver (who has moved on to greater fame as a political analyst), consists of three parts:

1. Major-league equivalencies, which use minor-league statistics to project how a player will perform in the major leagues;
2. Baseline forecasts, which use weighted averages and regression to the mean to estimate a player's current true talent level; and
3. Aging curves, which uses the career paths of comparable players to estimate how a player's statistics are likely to change over time.

With all those important things covered, let's take a look at what's in the book this year.

Team Prospectus

Most of this book is composed of team chapters, with one for each of the 30 major-league franchises. On the first page of each chapter, you'll see a box that contains some of the key statistics for each team as well as a very inviting stadium diagram. (You can see an example of this for the Milwaukee Brewers on this very page!)

We start with the team name, their unadjusted 2019 win-loss record, and their divisional ranking. Beneath that are a host of other team statistics. **Pythag** presents an adjusted 2019 winning percentage, calculated by taking runs scored per game (**RS/G**) and runs allowed per game (**RA/G**) for the team, and running them through a version of Bill James' Pythagorean formula that was refined and improved by David Smyth and Brandon Heipp. (The formula is called "Pythagenpat," which is equally fun to type and to say.)

Next up is **DRC+**, described earlier, to indicate the overall hitting ability of the team either above or below league-average. Run prevention on the pitching side is covered by **DRA** (also mentioned earlier) and another metric: Fielding Independent Pitching (**FIP**), which calculates another ERA-like statistic based on strikeouts, walks, and home runs recorded. Defensive Efficiency Rating (**DER**) tells us the percentage of balls in play turned into outs for the team, and is a quick fielding shorthand that rounds out run prevention.

After that, we have several measures related to roster composition, as opposed to on-field performance. **B-Age** and **P-Age** tell us the average age of a team's batters and pitchers, respectively. **Salary** is the combined team payroll for all on-field players, and Doug Pappas' Marginal Dollars per Marginal Win (**M$/MW**) tells us how much money a team spent to earn production above replacement level.

Ending this batch of statistics is the number of disabled list days a team had over the season (**IL Days**) and the amount of salary paid to players on the disabled list (**$ on IL**); this final number is expressed as a percentage of total payroll.

Next to each of these stats, we've listed each team's MLB rank in that category from first to 30th. In this, first always indicates a positive outcome and 30th a negative outcome, except in the case of salary—first is highest.

After the franchise statistics, we share a few items about the team's home ballpark. There's the aforementioned diagram of the park's dimensions (including distances to the outfield wall), a graphic showing the height of the wall from the left-field pole to the right-field pole, and a table showing three-year park factors for the stadium. The park factors are displayed as indexes where 100 is average, 110 means that the park inflates the statistic in question by 10 percent, and 90 means that the park deflates the statistic in question by 10 percent.

On the second page of each team chapter, you'll find three graphs. The first is the **2019 Hit List Ranking**. This shows our Hit List Rank for the team on each day of the 2019 season and is intended to give you a picture of the ups and downs of the team's season. Hit List Rank measures overall team performance and drives the Hit List Power Rankings at the baseballprospectus.com website.

The second graph is **Committed Payroll** and helps you see how the team's payroll has compared to the MLB and divisional average payrolls over time. Payroll figures are current as of January 1, 2020; with so many free agents still unsigned as of this writing, the final 2020 figure will likely be significantly different for many teams. (In the meantime, you can always find the most current data at Baseball Prospectus' Cot's Baseball Contracts page.)

The third graph is **Farm System Ranking** and displays how the Baseball Prospectus prospect team has ranked the organization's farm system since 2007.

After the graphs, we have a **Personnel** section that lists many of the important decision-makers and upper-level field and operations staff members for the franchise, as well as any former Baseball Prospectus staff members who are currently part of the organization. (In very rare circumstances, someone might be on both lists!)

Juan Soto LF

Born: 10/25/98   Age: 21   Bats: L   Throws: L
Height: 6'1"   Weight: 185   Origin: International Free Agent, 2015

YEAR	TEAM	LVL	AGE	PA	R	2B	3B	HR	RBI	BB	K	SB	CS	AVG/OBP/SLG
2017	NAT	RK	18	27	3	1	1	0	4	2	1	0	0	.320/.370/.440
2017	HAG	A	18	96	15	5	0	3	14	10	8	1	2	.360/.427/.523
2018	HAG	A	19	74	12	5	3	5	24	14	13	2	0	.373/.486/.814
2018	POT	A+	19	73	17	3	1	7	18	11	8	0	1	.371/.466/.790
2018	HAR	AA	19	35	4	2	0	2	10	4	7	1	0	.323/.400/.581
2018	WAS	MLB	19	494	77	25	1	22	70	79	99	5	2	.292/.406/.517
2019	WAS	MLB	20	659	110	32	5	34	110	108	132	12	1	.282/.401/.548
2020	WAS	MLB	21	630	92	30	3	35	102	85	123	5	2	.284/.382/.543

Comparables: Ronald Acuña Jr., Mike Trout, Tony Conigliaro

YEAR	TEAM	LVL	AGE	PA	DRC+	VORP	BABIP	BRR	FRAA	WARP
2017	NAT	RK	18	27	135	1.5	.333	0.0	RF(9): -1.1	0.0
2017	HAG	A	18	96	181	8.0	.373	1.0	RF(19): -1.9, LF(2): -0.3	0.9
2018	HAG	A	19	74	222	14.5	.405	0.3	RF(14): 1.1, CF(2): 0.2	1.2
2018	POT	A+	19	73	260	15.4	.340	1.4	RF(14): 1.0, LF(1): 0.0	1.6
2018	HAR	AA	19	35	113	3.6	.364	0.0	LF(4): 0.6, RF(4): -0.5	0.1
2018	WAS	MLB	19	494	125	40.5	.338	-0.5	LF(114): 2.7	3.0
2019	WAS	MLB	20	659	136	49.0	.312	1.4	LF(150): -0.8	4.9
2020	WAS	MLB	21	630	133	43.6	.310	-0.1	LF 3	4.8

Position Players

After all that information and a thoughtful bylined essay covering each team, we present our player comments. These are also bylined, but due to frequent franchise shifts during the offseason, our bylines are more a rough guide than a perfect accounting of who wrote what.

Each player is listed with the major-league team that employed him as of early January 2020. If a player changed teams after that point via free agency, trade, or any other method, you'll be able to find them in the chapter for their previous squad.

As an example, take a look at the player comment for Nationals outfielder Juan Soto: the stat block that accompanies his written comment is at the top of this page. First we cover biographical information (age is as of June 30, 2020) before moving onto the stats themselves. Our statistic columns include standard identifying information like **YEAR**, **TEAM**, **LVL** (level of affiliated play) and **AGE** before getting into the numbers. Next, we provide raw, untranslated numbers like you might find on the back of your dad's baseball cards: **PA** (plate appearances), **R** (runs), **2B** (doubles), **3B** (triples), **HR** (home runs), **RBI** (runs batted in), **BB** (walks), **K** (strikeouts), **SB** (stolen bases) and **CS** (caught stealing).

Next, we have unadjusted "slash" statistics: **AVG** (batting average), **OBP** (on-base percentage) and **SLG** (slugging percentage). Following the slash line is **DRC+** (Deserved Runs Created Plus), which we described earlier as total offensive expected contribution compared to the league average.

One of our oldest active metrics, **VORP** (Value Over Replacement Player), considers offensive production, position and plate appearances. In essence, it is the number of runs contributed beyond what a replacement-level player at the same position would contribute if given the same percentage of team plate appearances. VORP does not consider the quality of a player's defense.

BABIP (batting average on balls in play) tells us how often a ball in play fell for a hit, and can help us identify whether a batter may have been lucky or not...but note that high BABIPs also tend to follow the great hitters of our time, as well as speedy singles hitters who put the ball on the ground.

The next item is **BRR** (Baserunning Runs), which covers all of a player's baserunning accomplishments including (but not limited to) swiped bags and failed attempts. Next is **FRAA** (Fielding Runs Above Average), which also includes the number of games previously played at each position noted in parentheses. Multi-position players have only their two most frequent positions listed here, but their total FRAA number reflects all positions played.

Our last column here is **WARP** (Wins Above Replacement Player). WARP estimates the total value of a player, which means for hitters it takes into account hitting runs above average (calculated using the DRC+ model), BRR and FRAA. Then, it makes an adjustment for positions played and gives the player a credit for plate appearances based upon the difference between "replacement level"—which is derived from the quality of players added to a team's roster after the start of the season–and the league average.

The final line just below the stats box is **PECOTA** data, which is discussed further in a following section.

Catchers

Catchers are a special breed, and thus they have earned their own separate box which displays some of the defensive metrics that we've built just for them. As an example, let's check out J.T. Realmuto.

The **YEAR** and **TEAM** columns match what you'd find in the other stat box. **P. COUNT** indicates the number of pitches thrown while the catcher was behind the plate, including swinging strikes, fouls and balls in play. **FRM RUNS** is the total run value the catcher provided (or cost) his team by influencing the umpire to call strikes where other catchers did not. **BLK RUNS** expresses the total run value above or below average for the catcher's ability to prevent wild pitches and passed balls. **THRW RUNS** is calculated using a similar model as the previous two statistics, and it measures a catcher's ability to throw out basestealers but also to dissuade them from testing his arm in the first place. It takes into account factors like the pitcher (including his delivery and pickoff move) and baserunner (who could be as fast as Billy Hamilton or as slow as Yonder Alonso). **TOT RUNS** is the sum of all of the previous three statistics.

Justin Verlander RHP
Born: 02/20/83   Age: 37   Bats: R   Throws: R
Height: 6'5"   Weight: 225   Origin: Round 1, 2004 Draft (#2 overall)

YEAR	TEAM	LVL	AGE	W	L	SV	G	GS	IP	H	HR	BB/9	K/9	K	GB%	BABIP
2017	DET	MLB	34	10	8	0	28	28	172	153	23	3.5	9.2	176	34%	.283
2017	HOU	MLB	34	5	0	0	5	5	34	17	4	1.3	11.4	43	32%	.194
2018	HOU	MLB	35	16	9	0	34	34	214	156	28	1.6	12.2	290	31%	.272
2019	HOU	MLB	36	21	6	0	34	34	223	137	36	1.7	12.1	300	36%	.219
2020	HOU	MLB	37	15	6	0	29	29	184	138	28	2.3	12.1	248	35%	.274

Comparables: Zack Greinke, A.J. Burnett, Aníbal Sánchez

YEAR	TEAM	LVL	AGE	WHIP	ERA	DRA	WARP	MPH	FB%	WHF	CSP
2017	DET	MLB	34	1.28	3.82	4.03	3.0	97.7	58	11	47.8
2017	HOU	MLB	34	0.65	1.06	3.08	0.9	97.5	59.6	15.1	49.9
2018	HOU	MLB	35	0.90	2.52	2.33	7.3	97.5	61.2	16.2	51.6
2019	HOU	MLB	36	0.80	2.58	2.51	7.9	96.8	49.9	17.5	48.3
2020	HOU	MLB	37	1.01	2.75	2.95	5.3	95.8	54.6	15.1	48.2

Pitchers

Let's give our pitchers a turn, using 2019 AL Cy Young winner Justin Verlander as our example. Take a look at his stat block: the first line and the **YEAR**, **TEAM**, **LVL** and **AGE** columns are the same as in the position player example earlier.

Here too, we have a series of columns that display raw, unadjusted statistics compiled by the pitcher over the course of a season: **W** (wins), **L** (losses), **SV** (saves), **G** (games pitched), **GS** (games started), **IP** (innings pitched), **H** (hits allowed) and **HR** (home runs allowed). Next we have two statistics that are rates: **BB/9** (walks per nine innings) and **K/9** (strikeouts per nine innings), before returning to the unadjusted K (strikeouts).

Next up is **GB%** (ground ball percentage), which is the percentage of all batted balls that were hit on the ground, including both outs and hits. Remember, this is based on observational data and subject to human error, so please approach this with a healthy dose of skepticism.

BABIP (batting average on balls in play) is calculated using the same methodology as it is for position players, but it often tells us more about a pitcher than it does a hitter. With pitchers, a high BABIP is often due to poor defense or bad luck, and can often be an indicator of potential rebound, and a low BABIP may be cause to expect performance regression. (A typical league-average BABIP is close to .290-.300.)

Texas Rangers 2020

The metrics **WHIP** (walks plus hits per inning pitched) and **ERA** (earned run average) are old standbys: WHIP measures walks and hits allowed on a per-inning basis, while ERA measures earned runs on a nine-inning basis. Neither of these stats are translated or adjusted.

DRA (Deserved Run Average) was described at length earlier, and measures how many runs the pitcher "deserved" to allow per nine innings. Please note that since we lack all the data points that would make for a "real" DRA for minor-league events, the DRA displayed for minor league partial-seasons is based off of different data. (That data is a modified version of our cFIP metric, which you can find more information about on our website.)

Just like with hitters, **WARP** (Wins Above Replacement Player) is a total value metric that puts pitchers of all stripes on the same scale as position players. We use DRA as the primary input for our calculation of WARP. You might notice that relief pitchers (due to their limited innings) may have a lower WARP than you were expecting or than you might see in other WARP-like metrics. WARP does not take leverage into account, just the actions a pitcher performs and the expected value of those actions...which ends up judging high-leverage relief pitchers differently than you might imagine given their prestige and market value.

MPH gives you the pitcher's 95th percentile velocity for the noted season, in order to give you an idea of what the *peak* fastball velocity a pitcher possesses. Since this comes from our pitch-tracking data, it is not publicly available for minor-league pitchers.

Finally, we display the three new pitching metrics we described earlier. **FB%** (fastball percentage) gives you the percentage of fastballs thrown out of all pitches. **WHF** (whiff rate) tells you the percentage of swinging strikes induced out of all pitches. **CSP** (called strike probability) expresses the likelihood of all pitches thrown to result in a called strike, after controlling for factors like handedness, umpire, pitch type, count and location.

PECOTA

All players have PECOTA projections for 2020, as well as a set of other numbers that describe the performance of comparable players according to PECOTA. All projections for 2020 are for the player at the date we went to press in early January and are projected into the league and park context as indicated by the team abbreviation. (Note that players at very low levels of the minors are too unpredictable to assess using these numbers.) All PECOTA projected statistics represent a player's projected major-league performance.

Below the projections are the player's three highest-scoring comparable players as determined by PECOTA. All comparables represent a snapshot of how the listed player was performing at the same age as the current player, so if a

23-year-old pitcher is compared to Bartolo Colón, he's actually being compared to a 23-year-old Colón, not the version that pitched for the Rangers in 2018, nor to Colón's career as a whole.

A few points about pitcher projections. First, we aren't yet projecting peak velocity, so that column will be blank in the PECOTA lines. Second, projecting DRA is trickier than evaluating past performance, because it is unclear how deserving each pitcher will be of his anticipated outcomes. However, we know that another DRA-related statistic–contextual FIP or cFIP-estimates future run scoring very well. So for PECOTA, the projected DRA figures you see are based on the past cFIPs generated by the pitcher and comparable players over time, along with the other factors described above.

Lineouts

In each chapter's Lineouts section, you'll find abbreviated text comments, as well as all the same information you'd find in our full player comments. The only difference is that we limit the stats boxes in this section to only including the 2019 information for each player.

Managers

After all those wonderful team chapters, we've got statistics for each big-league manager, all of whom are organized by alphabetical order. Here you'll find a block including an extraordinary amount of information collected from each manager's entire career. For more information on the acronyms and what they mean, please visit the Glossary at www.baseballprospectus.com.

There is one important metric that we'd like to call attention to, and you'll find it next to each manager's name: **wRM+** (weighted reliever management plus). Developed by Rob Arthur and Rian Watt, wRM+ investigates how good a manager is at using their best relievers during the moments of highest leverage, using both our proprietary DRA metric as well as Leverage Index. wRM+ is scaled to a league average of 100, and a wRM+ of 105 indicates that relievers were used approximately five percent "better" than average. On the other hand, a wRM+ of 95 would tell us the team used its relievers five percent "worse" than the average team.

While wRM+ does not have an extremely strong correlation with a manager, it is statistically significant; this means that a manager is not *entirely* responsible for a team's wRM+, but does have some effect on that number.

PECOTA Leaderboards

If you're familiar with PECOTA, then you'll have noticed that the projection system often appears bullish on players coming off a bad year and bearish on players coming off a good year. (This is because the system weights several previous seasons, not just the most recent one.) In addition, we publish the 50th

Texas Rangers 2020

percentile projections for each player–which is smack in the middle of the range of projected production—which tends to mean PECOTA stat lines don't often have extreme results like 40 home runs or 250 strikeouts in a given season. In essence, PECOTA doesn't project very many extreme seasons.

At the end of the book, we've ranked the top players at each position based on their PECOTA projections. This might help you visualize just how a given player's projection compares to that of their peers, so that even if a dramatic stat line isn't projected, you can still imagine how they stack up against the rest of the league.

Part 1: Team Analysis

Texas Rangers: Where Are You Going, Where Have You Been?

Ben Carsley, Samuel Hale and Matthew Trueblood

2019: What Went Right
The end result—the Rangers being a losing team—isn't very surprising. Yet, one could argue that the Rangers have been a bit more interesting and entertaining than your standard average-ish team, proof that the journey can be more rewarding than the destination. The Rangers were 10 games above .500 as late as June 28. It was already clear that they wouldn't be winning the division thanks to their intrastate rivals, but for a solid 50 percent of the 2019 season, Rangers fans had a reason to believe their team could play in the postseason.

It feels silly to start anywhere other than the pitching, and by the pitching we pretty much mean Lance Lynn and Mike Minor exclusively. You'd be forgiven for not expecting much out of this suddenly dynamic duo when the season began. Instead, both Lynn and Minor enjoyed the best seasons of their careers. Lynn finished eighth in the majors in WARP and 16th in DRA- while Minor was 30th and 39th, respectively. Neither pitcher is likely to sustain at this level, but they were incontrovertibly "right" in 2019. And that just about sums up the good news on the pitching front.

The Rangers saw some of their young hitters take steps forward. Joey Gallo has emerged as one of the game's preeminent (if oft-injured) sluggers, posting the best DRC+ of his career. Willie Calhoun's turbulent Rangers career finally leveled out long enough for him to establish himself as a major leaguer. Danny Santana came out of nowhere to serve as a useful chess piece all over the diamond, and Nick Solak looks ready to follow suit. Shin-Soo Choo and Elvis Andrus keep on chugging. There are some building blocks here.

Undoubtedly the Most Fun Ranger Award of 2019 belonged to Hunter Pence. All but left for dead by the general baseball intelligentsia, Pence signed a one-year, $2 million contract for his age-36 season. Though injuries limited his playing time, when he was available he was, somewhat inexplicably, better than he had been in years—his 122 DRC+ was his best since 2011.

2019: What Went Wrong

While the Rangers got surprise performances from some of their veteran players, they were also let down by several parts of their young core. A few years ago, it seemed reasonable to believe that Nomar Mazara and Rougned Odor would serve as the faces of the franchise, the pillars upon which the Next Great Rangers Team would rest. Neither player has capitalized on their potential. Mazara looks like a role-5 corner outfielder at best, and while was still only 24, we now have more than 2,000 PA from him that tell us not to expect stardom. Odor has reverted to his 2017 level of non-production, which is not great considering he's going to get more expensive (if still fairly affordable) over the next three seasons of his contract extension.

Elsewhere, Ronald Guzmán and Delino DeShields proved yet again that they should not be starters on contending teams. The Rangers also gave Jeff Mathis in excess of 240 plate appearances. His OPS+ sits at 11. Great defense or not, at some point, this has to stop.

Yet for as many hiccups as the Rangers experienced in the lineup, they were even more plagued by their age-old nemesis; pitching. To Lynn and Minor we might add José Leclerc, who rebounded nicely from a rough start to the season. But you'd be hard-pressed to find another arm on this team worth much of a damn. Ariel Jurado started the third-most games for the Rangers (18) and his DRA was 7.21. Next up was Adrian Sampson (15) who topped him, in a backwards sort of way, with a DRA of 7.49. Other Rangers starters have included Brock Burke, Kolby Allard, Jesse Chavez, Shelby Miller, and Drew Smyly. None save Chavez has been even remotely effective, and Chavez was ruled out for the year with an elbow issue in August. As such, he had the best September among the arms that were just listed.

Sure, pitchers like Yohander Méndez, Emmanuel Clase, and Brett Martin emerged as tolerable bullpen pieces, but in general this organization is totally bereft of pitching talent ready to contribute at the MLB level outside the two veterans who headline its rotation and the closer they probably overpaid last offseason. Clase was subsequently sent to Cleveland (along with DeShields) in return for Corey Kluber and cash. If Kluber can rebound, he'll help, but he was available at a discount for a reason. —*Ben Carsley*

Prospect Outlook

Advancement was a major theme of the Rangers farm this season. At the top end, a couple carloads of pitchers found their way to Arlington. It was a nice mix of starters such as Burke, Joe Palumbo, and Allard and relievers like Clase, Jonathan Hernández, and Martin. They also cashed in one lotto ticket success in Pete Fairbanks for a potentially longer-lasting impact in **Nick Solak**. Mix that in with a heavy dose of Willie Calhoun finally sticking at the big-league level while hitting everything within arm's grasp, and the youth movement is on.

There was plenty below deck to keep prospect nerds excited. Righties **Tyler Phillips** and **Jason Bahr** continued their ascents upward at Double-A, joined by top prospect **Leody Taveras**, who could be—at the very least—a star defensive center fielder. A bonded pair of burly relievers, **Joe Barlow** and **Demarcus Evans**, also blazed up from Single-A with Barlow cracking Triple-A. The real mojo however came in the lower ranks, with a lot of names pushing themselves forward. Right-hander **Cole Winn** shook off inconsistency to show his form as a former top draft pick. Third baseman **Sherten Apostel**, one of two players in the Keone Kela trade, found his way from relative obscurity to likely top ten status by hitting everything that moved. **Hans Crouse** kept people aware of his presence simply by existing, but his future as a starter or reliever is still to be decided. Third baseman **Josh Jung** arrived via the first round of the draft and performed so well he ended up in full-season ball.

Those are just the major names. It's all remarkable because of how far the system has come since it was slashed and burned for a title that never came. Now it's robust, bulging at the seams with talent just waiting for time to grow and more chances to display said growth. This is what advancement looks like, and it's beautiful.

As for a major 2020 contributor out of this wide group, keep your eyes on Evans. He's a mountain of a man with a great nickname (the Mississippi Mean), a two-pitch mix of fastball and curveball all coming from a high release point. His command is the sticky widget that might prevent this from happening. Nevertheless, this is your warning big-league hitters: The Mississippi Mean is coming, and you're probably not ready. —*Samuel Hale*

2020 Outlook

It feels like almost an entire decade in Arlington has unfolded in the long shadow of the two pennant-winning teams in 2010 and 2011 and the famous farm system the Rangers assembled even as they kept winning. That hangover is finally starting to fade. Mazara became the next former phenom to leave town when Jon Daniels shipped him to the White Sox. The promising homegrown arms to which the team wed itself for years have busted, been traded, or left as free agents, so after Minor and Lynn rewarded prior forays into the starter market, the Rangers double-dipped in that bowl this time, plucking Kyle Gibson and Jordan Lyles on multi-year deals.

The club did try to court higher-profile free agents, including Anthony Rendon and Josh Donaldson. The prices for the top talent proved too rich for their tastes, though, so Texas made reasonable, solid investments further down the chain. Todd Frazier will man third base and formerly estranged son Robinson Chirinos gives the team a much-needed offensive boost behind the plate. Joely Rodríguez, who made a sojourn in Japan, came back Stateside and landed in the Texas bullpen.

Texas Rangers 2020

The flip side of the affordability of backend rotation additions and second-division positional regulars, of course, is that their upside is limited. Lyles or Gibson could take a Lynn-style leap forward, but it seems less likely in each case than it was for Lynn. Thus, Corey Kluber stands out as the big move Daniels made. Kluber could be the game-changer, doing more than chewing up innings and keeping the team in games—as long as he stays healthy and his apparent decline in last season's small sample doesn't prove to be the start of an ugly slide. The Rangers aren't necessarily young, but this is beginning to be a new-look team befitting its brand-new ballpark. —*Matthew Trueblood*

Performance Graphs

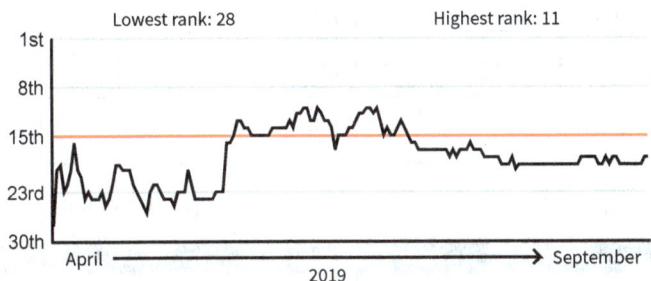

2019 Hit List Ranking

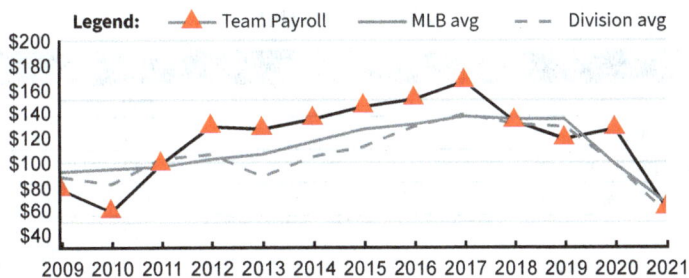

Committed Payroll (in millions)

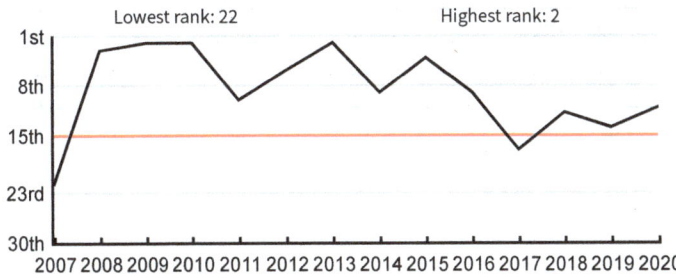

Farm System Ranking

2019 Team Performance

ACTUAL STANDINGS

Team	W	L	Pct
HOU	107	55	0.660
OAK	97	65	0.599
TEX	**78**	**84**	**0.481**
LAA	72	90	0.444
SEA	68	94	0.420

THIRD-ORDER STANDINGS

Team	W	L	Pct
HOU	117	45	0.719
OAK	95	67	0.584
LAA	73	89	0.453
SEA	72	90	0.444
TEX	**71**	**91**	**0.437**

TOP HITTERS

Player	WARP
Joey Gallo	2.6
Elvis Andrus	2.4
Danny Santana	2.1

TOP PITCHERS

Player	WARP
Lance Lynn	5.9
Mike Minor	3.9
José Leclerc	1.8

VITAL STATISTICS

Statistic Name	Value	Rank
Pythagenpat	.460	18th
Runs Scored per Game	4.99	12th
Runs Allowed per Game	5.42	25th
Deserved Runs Created Plus	94	17th
Deserved Run Average	5.42	23rd
Fielding Independent Pitching	4.87	23rd
Defensive Efficiency Rating	.688	27th
Batter Age	28.8	24th
Pitcher Age	28.2	18th
Salary	$118.3M	20th
Marginal $ per Marginal Win	$3.6M	17th
Injured List Days	1423	25th
$ on IL	7%	1st

2020 Team Projections

PROJECTED STANDINGS

Team	W	L	Pct	+/-
HOU	98.3	63.7	0.607	-9
LAA	86.8	75.2	0.536	15
OAK	84.6	77.4	0.522	-12
TEX	**73.0**	**89.0**	**0.451**	**-5**
SEA	66.0	96.0	0.407	-2

TOP PROJECTED HITTERS

Player	WARP
Joey Gallo	3.8
Elvis Andrus	1.5
Nick Solak	1.4

TOP PROJECTED PITCHERS

Player	WARP
Corey Kluber	2.4
Lance Lynn	2.2
Mike Minor	1.6

FARM SYSTEM REPORT

Top Prospect	Number of Top 101 Prospects
Leody Taveras, #37	3

KEY DEDUCTIONS

Player	WARP
Delino DeShields	0.8
Hunter Pence	0.7
Nate Jones	0.3
Logan Forsythe	0.1
Emmanuel Clase	0.1
Jeffrey Springs	0.0
Nomar Mazara	-0.1
CD Pelham	-0.1
Phillips Valdez	-0.2

KEY ADDITIONS

Player	WARP
Corey Kluber	2.4
Todd Frazier	0.8
Nick Goody	0.5
Kyle Gibson	0.5
Sherten Apostel	0.4
Demarcus Evans	0.3
Jordan Lyles	0.3
Matt Duffy	0.2
Robinson Chirinos	0.1
Greg Bird	0.0

Team Personnel

President of Baseball Operations & General Manager
Jon Daniels

Assistant General Manager
Josh Boyd

Assistant General Manager
Mike Daly

Assistant General Manager
Shiraz Rehman

Manager
Chris Woodward

BP Alumni
Bradley Ankrom
Andrew Koo

Globe Life Park in Arlington Stats

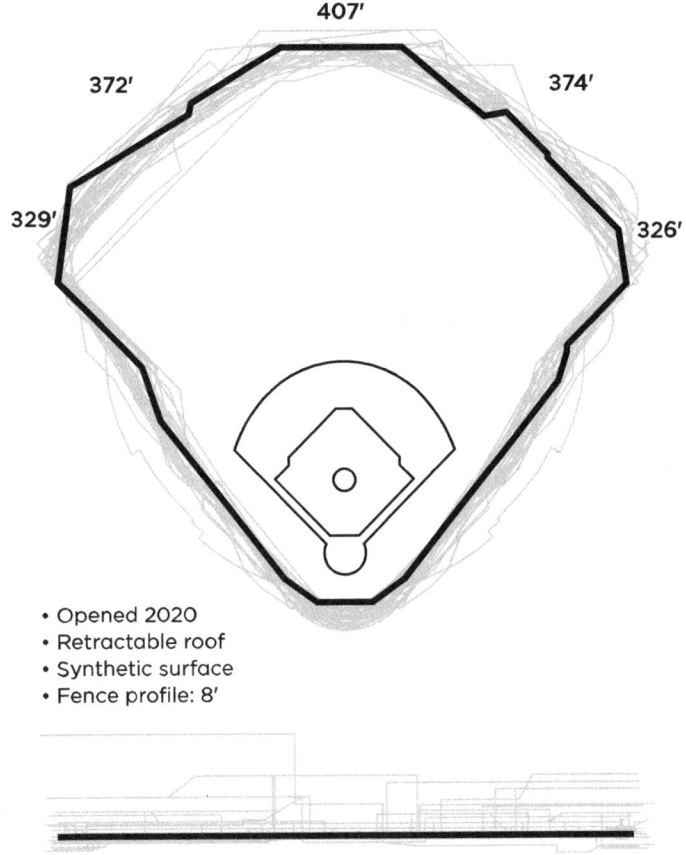

- Opened 2020
- Retractable roof
- Synthetic surface
- Fence profile: 8'

Three-Year Park Factors

Runs	Runs/RH	Runs/LH	HR/RH	HR/LH
109	108	111	103	106

Rangers Team Analysis

The Rangers are opening a new ballpark this spring. It will be across the street from the old one, the one that opened 26 years ago and hosted the franchise's greatest period of success. Its very name—Globe Life Field—will give off a vibe that is more "spot-the-difference puzzle" than "heralding a new era." It will have a retractable roof to shelter the masses from sweltering summer heat; that's the big difference. Reading about it, you'd swear a law had been passed requiring the old, retiring stadium to be described as a "perfectly good ballpark." This is Texas, though; epicenter of a distinctive type of performative wealth—Southfork, oil barons, Mark Cuban, etc.

The thriving dad down the street replaces his SUV with the latest model every two years, without fail. A bigger swimming pool plants itself in the ground across the way. And yes, your instincts are right: Jerry Jones did build that other stadium in town at least partially as a monument to his personal largesse. Perfectly good isn't nearly as good as brand stinkin' new and declaratively expensive. Why live comfortably when you could live in luxury?

Pursuit of extravagance is not particularly stirring or sympathetic as life credos go, but within the context of sports fandom, it's the dream. Underlying the comfort and companionship of baseball's day-to-day grind is the same invitation other televised, professional athletic endeavors extend: A chance to fall back on our more base instincts, winners, losers. Champions. Count the wins, count the rings, and flaunt it. All the superiority for the cost of a T-shirt, a certain color cap, or the simple fact of being born in one town over the other.

Since baseball's current Collective Bargaining Agreement took effect in 2017 it has often felt that the league's owners are intentionally suppressing their own thirst for being the best, and depriving fans of the vicarious thrill of achieving it. Using a luxury tax, now known by the infinitely more bureaucratic and sinister Competitive Balance Tax as one important cudgel, those in power have made clear that there are (artificially) fewer things to spend on, fewer outwardly exciting investments worthy of a front office's attention and fewer incentives to vault past "perfectly good."

They have reframed success as the art of getting by.

And while some clubs have fielded more winners by diving headlong into this more arcane mode of building a team, the Rangers have not. Either by unfortunate circumstance or lacking aptitude, they have been slow to find precious stars in development and youth. Instead, they have constructed an urgent case for chasing the gaudy, luxurious new thing.

⚾   ⚾   ⚾

The Texas Rangers, once upon a time, backed up the Brinks truck to strike the first Alex Rodriguez deal. As defending American League champs after 2010, they saw franchise third baseman Michael Young and raised themselves Adrián Beltré to the tune of $96 million and great interpersonal strife. (Young requested a trade, feeling betrayed and marginalized, but ultimately remained with the club in 2011 and scratched out 689 plate appearances, a majors-leading 213 hits and one admittedly strange first-place MVP vote.)

That same summer, they spent $4.95 million to sign a 16-year-old international prospect of great promise named Nomar Mazara and another $3.45 million on a 16-year-old named Ronald Guzmán in a fit of what turned out to be transitional "extravagance"—Mazara's bonus alone would be larger than the average team's entire international pool, as dictated by the current CBA.

As Beltré's time in Texas unspooled, players like Mazara, Guzmán and international classmate Rougned Odor made it to the majors, as did 2012 draftee Joey Gallo. But with the last big splash fading into retirement, GM Jon Daniels' strong record of useful acquisitions has been largely overshadowed by the organization's struggle to turn those homegrown players into an actual winning core.

This is not to call them cheap or cynical. Even during a relatively clear stretch of rebuilding/retooling, the Rangers signed veterans to fill holes instead of letting open sores weep through the summer simply to accrue better draft picks.

Still, the young, sustainable, successful core has not come to fruition. Or maybe the young and sustainable has. The successful, not so much. At 6-foot-4 and not quite 21 years old, Mazara screamed promise when he arrived in 2016. Occasional 500-foot home runs into the now-defunct ballpark's steep right-field seats piled on to the aura of potential, but four seasons of slightly below average offensive lines—evidently very sustainable—from a corner outfield spot dampened that hope and weighed down the lineup.

Originally signed for less than one-tenth of Mazara's bonus, the fact that Rougned Odor reached the big leagues at all was a win. That he played a supporting role in perhaps the wildest inning in recent baseball history and later claimed the sport's pound-for-pound punching title counts as gravy, to be honest.

His ongoing presence in the order, however, is becoming hard to stomach. In only one of the last three seasons has he even sniffed average offensive production, and in 2017 and 2019 he logged "absolute wizard of a shortstop" level DRC+ numbers (75 and 87, respectively) despite hitting 30 homers in each season. Whether it's commitment to a still-young player who displayed promise as a 20-year-old rookie or something else, there are fewer and fewer arguments available in favor of Odor tallying 500 at-bats for a team trying to compete. At present, he's a walking, talking manifestation of a fact that baseball keeps teaching us: If you limit your choices to all or nothing, you'll usually wind up bitter and disillusioned that there is far more nothing in the world.

Still, in the midst of the nothing, there are often flickers. Every year, including this past one, Odor teases hopeful hearts and minds with a scorch-your-eyebrows-off hot streak. The 2019 version involved a .648 September slugging percentage, but the dark side of this streakiness is more prevalent. Just since the start of 2017, the Rangers have allowed Odor to slog through five different calendar months of at least 80 plate appearances with batting averages below .200—a terrifying display of faith only exceeded by his nemesis, José Bautista, in twilight, along with entrenched veterans Curtis Granderson and Kole Calhoun.

They won't stand accused of being too quick-tempered with their young, cost-controlled players. There is, of course, one tale of patience that appears to be paying off: Gallo—he of the prodigious power but flighty contact skills—legitimately took off under new manager Chris Woodward and a shifting coaching staff in 2019. He connected for 22 homers in only 70 games, yes. He also pared back his swing rate to about 40 percent, allowing more bad pitches to go by and bolster his on-base percentage to a star-level .389.

But even granting that they have pushed money into better player development practices that could produce further Gallo-like leaps, the present-day Rangers can't hang their hat there. Consider where their production came from in 2019.

2019 WARP DEVELOPED		2019 WARP ACQUIRED	
1.5		16.1	
PLAYER	2019 WARP	PLAYER	2019 WARP
Joey Gallo	2.6	Lance Lynn	5.9
Elvis Andrus	2.4	Mike Minor	3.9
José Leclerc	1.8	Danny Santana	2.1
Brad Martin	0.6	Shin-Soo Choo	2.0
Emmanuel Clase	0.4	Asdrúbal Cabrera	1.8
José Trevino	0.3	Hunter Pence	1.7
Ronald Guzmán	0.3	Delino DeShields	1.4
Peter Fairbanks	0.2	Willie Calhoun	1.1
Nomar Mazara	0.1	Chris Martin	0.9
Others	-7.2	Others	-4.7

Players acquired for immediate or near-immediate contributions in Arlington accumulated 16.1 WARP. The group of players whose development can be more reasonably credited to the Rangers was worth…1.5 WARP, and that's with Gallo alone notching 2.6 WARP. (Willie Calhoun is the one confusing case. If you're so inclined to grant his WARP to the development side, I won't argue.)

So even as much of the energy in the industry flows toward developing young talent, this team seems to be better the more directly and overtly Daniels and company assemble it from imported parts.

⚾ ⚾ ⚾

Even in the hole-plugging, water-treading days of 2019, outside additions thrived in Texas. In the second season of his three-year, $29 million deal, Mike Minor took off. Employing a four-pitch mix and amping up the usage of his bendy changeup, the lefty more than validated the decision to convert him back to the rotation.

Then there was Lance Lynn, who signed a three-year, $30 million deal that seemed to say, "Let's try the Mike Minor trick again!" This went about as well as it possibly could. Lynn found an extra gear of strikeout potential in his four-seamer and went from innings-eating starter to Cy Young contender.

Twin mini-risks on veteran arms—Lynn could certainly be called established while Minor was still ramping back up from an injury—turned into twin jackpots, and it's hard to overstate how bad the pitching would have been even if they were simply their old selves. Rangers starters had a 5.37 ERA despite 416 2/3 combined innings of stellar work from Minor and Lynn.

Other, even smaller moves also had strong enough hit rates for Daniels & Co. While Asdrúbal Cabrera and Logan Forsythe proved modest disappointments, the Hunter Pence flier netted a .910 OPS. Danny Santana (?) wound up churning out 511 plate appearances of an .857 OPS (?!).

All of which raised the question: Why not at least try to translate that hit rate into more ambitious upgrades?

In this winter of increased activity, the Rangers appear intent on doing that. They moved on from Mazara and opened a permanent space for Gallo. They continued with the $30 million-ish rotation filler bets that could turn into something more, adding Kyle Gibson, Jordan Lyles, and Joely Rodríguez. Crucially, they also swooped in for Corey Kluber via trade and appeared eager to spend elsewhere (though not eager enough to keep potential Beltré heir Anthony Rendon from joining a division rival).

The shorthand, as spring draws near, will go like this: The Rangers are gearing up to field a stronger product to capitalize on their new ballpark. Its roof will keep the air down to a more pleasant temperature in the upper 70s, even in the sweltering Texas summer. And the team will try to break its win total out of the less pleasant upper 70s purgatory of recent years.

For all the ways money spent on players is framed around the norms of investments and hard choices, fans can and should remember that their team is not in danger of going bankrupt over the baseball equivalent of splurging for a fancier car. Sports exist to free them of those concerns—not burden them with those of a shadowy billionaire or two (Ray Davis and Bob Simpson, in the Rangers' case).

Fact is: the degree to which Lynn exceeded expectations in year one isn't all that different from the degree to which Beltré exceeded expectations across the length of his deal, and perhaps the Rangers have some skill in identifying players who will surprise. But $30 million gets you an enjoyable, day-making pitcher who surges to a fifth-place finish in Cy Young voting, whereas $96 million might affirm a fan's allegiance for life, and offer them the chance to watch a star become a Hall of Famer in their colors.

These aren't the only ways to upgrade a team. A Kyle Gibson or Jordan Lyles doesn't need to exceed expectations, for instance, to improve upon the fledgling starters of 2019 Rangers vintage. A competitor for Odor's playing time at second base doesn't have to be a star to level out the dizzying highs and lows of the position. Money spent on the technologies and smart employees that could turn more draftees into Gallo-style success stories is still worthwhile. It just hasn't and won't replicate the satisfaction of going and getting the best players just because you want the best players.

What stands between those two things is, yes, mostly just a billionaire's willingness to throw money around.

—*Zach Crizer is an author of Baseball Prospectus.*

Part 2: Player Analysis

PLAYER COMMENTS WITH GRAPHS

Elvis Andrus SS
Born: 08/26/88 Age: 31 Bats: R Throws: R
Height: 6'0" Weight: 200 Origin: International Free Agent, 2005

YEAR	TEAM	LVL	AGE	PA	R	2B	3B	HR	RBI	BB	K	SB	CS	AVG/OBP/SLG
2017	TEX	MLB	28	689	100	44	4	20	88	38	101	25	10	.297/.337/.471
2018	TEX	MLB	29	428	53	20	3	6	33	28	66	5	3	.256/.308/.367
2019	TEX	MLB	30	648	81	27	4	12	72	34	96	31	8	.275/.313/.393
2020	TEX	MLB	31	630	62	30	4	11	63	40	97	20	8	.267/.318/.389

Comparables: Tomas Perez, Edgar Renteria, Jack Wilson

The Rangers' elder statesman—not by age, but as the last standing member of the team to have played in the 2011 World Series—Andrus overcame a heartbreaking end of the 2015 season to have career years in 2016 and 2017, only to miss a large portion of 2018 due to a broken bone in his right elbow. That was super terrible timing for Andrus, who had the first of two opt-outs in his career after that season. He wasn't bad in 2019 before his second (and final) opt-out, but his numbers were more in line with his inconsistent early-career totals. Whether or not Andrus was going to stay in Texas anyway, we may never know, but in this timeline, it made sense to stick around and take the remainder of his paycheck over the next three (or four, pending plate appearances in 2021-22) years. If he can somehow find that 2017-18 gear again, his contract will be an absolute steal for the Rangers.

YEAR	TEAM	LVL	AGE	PA	DRC+	VORP	BABIP	BRR	FRAA	WARP
2017	TEX	MLB	28	689	108	37.7	.325	2.8	SS(157): 16.2	5.7
2018	TEX	MLB	29	428	91	9.2	.292	0.5	SS(97): -6.4	0.8
2019	TEX	MLB	30	648	89	21.8	.305	2.0	SS(146): 1.0	2.4
2020	TEX	MLB	31	630	85	12.2	.304	1.1	SS 3	1.5

Elvis Andrus, continued

Batted Ball Distribution

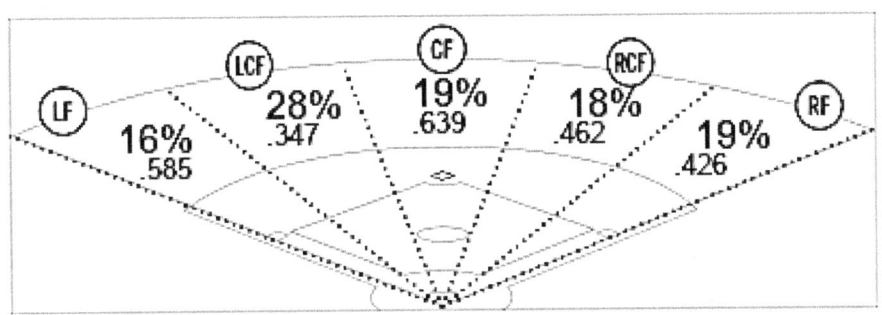

Strike Zone vs LHP   Strike Zone vs RHP

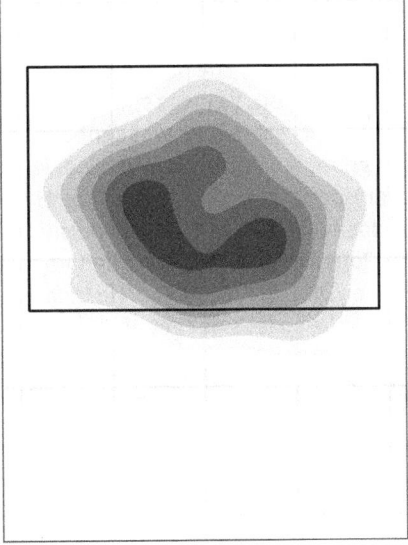

Willie Calhoun LF

Born: 11/04/94 Age: 25 Bats: L Throws: R
Height: 5'8" Weight: 187 Origin: Round 4, 2015 Draft (#132 overall)

YEAR	TEAM	LVL	AGE	PA	R	2B	3B	HR	RBI	BB	K	SB	CS	AVG/OBP/SLG
2017	OKL	AAA	22	414	64	24	5	23	67	36	49	3	2	.298/.357/.574
2017	ROU	AAA	22	120	16	3	1	8	26	6	12	1	0	.310/.345/.566
2017	TEX	MLB	22	37	3	0	0	1	4	2	7	0	0	.265/.324/.353
2018	ROU	AAA	23	470	66	32	0	9	47	32	47	4	0	.294/.351/.431
2018	TEX	MLB	23	108	8	5	0	2	11	6	24	0	0	.222/.269/.333
2019	NAS	AAA	24	172	23	8	0	8	28	32	24	1	1	.297/.433/.529
2019	TEX	MLB	24	337	51	14	1	21	48	23	53	0	0	.269/.323/.524
2020	TEX	MLB	25	560	73	28	1	30	87	46	99	1	0	.266/.331/.504

Comparables: Lonnie Chisenhall, Dave Collins, Kolten Wong

It's still unclear which was more shocking: Calhoun's off-season transformation that saw him report to spring training 26 pounds lighter than he left the team in 2018, or the fact that it (still) wasn't enough to land him a spot on the Opening Day roster. When he was recalled in May, it appeared the future had finally arrived—he hit .425 with an 1.197 OPS in his first six games—and then a strained left quad played the part of the evil plot twist. When Calhoun returned to action, he cooled a bit, but was still hitting .277 (.802) with only 19 strikeouts in 99 plate appearances when he was sent back to Triple-A yet again in July. That assignment was only about a week long, however, and Calhoun was an almost-every-day player upon returning. He tinkered a bit at second base while he was in Nashville, but with new acquisition Nick Solak now the primary competitor for Rougned Odor's job, it appears that Calhoun will be the team's regular left fielder/DH in 2020. Maybe. He technically does still have a minor-league option available, so let's not get ahead of ourselves.

YEAR	TEAM	LVL	AGE	PA	DRC+	VORP	BABIP	BRR	FRAA	WARP
2017	OKL	AAA	22	414	125	29.1	.289	-1.8	2B(74): 0.9, LF(12): -1.9	2.6
2017	ROU	AAA	22	120	130	10.0	.290	-1.2	LF(24): 2.4, 2B(3): -0.7	2.5
2017	TEX	MLB	22	37	87	1.0	.308	0.3	LF(11): -0.7	0.0
2018	ROU	AAA	23	470	118	14.3	.314	-3.2	LF(91): -11.9	0.6
2018	TEX	MLB	23	108	87	-2.5	.267	-0.7	LF(27): -2.8	-0.3
2019	NAS	AAA	24	172	141	18.1	.311	-0.8	LF(33): -6.5, 2B(3): 0.2	0.6
2019	TEX	MLB	24	337	119	17.3	.262	1.1	LF(71): -7.1	1.1
2020	TEX	MLB	25	560	114	24.9	.277	0.5	LF -10	1.5

Willie Calhoun, continued

Batted Ball Distribution

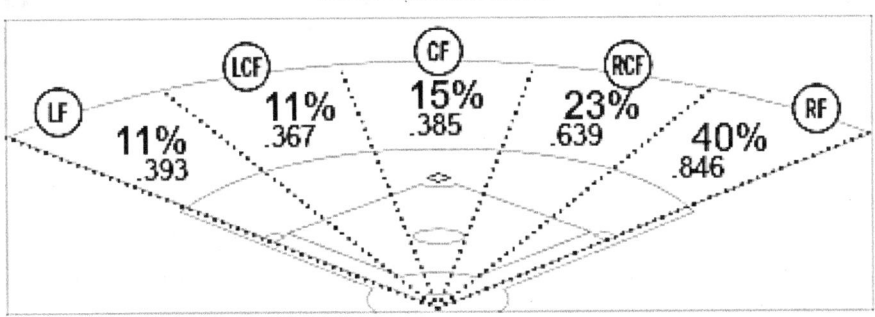

Strike Zone vs LHP   **Strike Zone vs RHP**

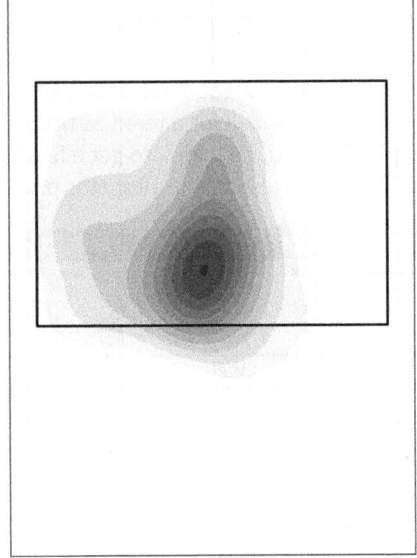

Robinson Chirinos C

Born: 06/05/84   Age: 36   Bats: R   Throws: R
Height: 6'1"   Weight: 210   Origin: International Free Agent, 2000

YEAR	TEAM	LVL	AGE	PA	R	2B	3B	HR	RBI	BB	K	SB	CS	AVG/OBP/SLG
2017	TEX	MLB	33	309	46	13	1	17	38	34	79	1	0	.255/.360/.506
2018	TEX	MLB	34	426	48	15	1	18	65	45	140	2	0	.222/.338/.419
2019	HOU	MLB	35	437	57	22	1	17	58	51	125	1	2	.238/.347/.443
2020	TEX	MLB	36	350	40	14	1	14	44	34	104	1	0	.212/.312/.399

Comparables: Adam Hyzdu, Dan Johnson, Mike Hegan

YEAR	TEAM	P. COUNT	FRM RUNS	BLK RUNS	THRW RUNS	TOT RUNS
2017	TEX	11679	-1.6	2.4	-0.9	0.2
2018	TEX	15072	-11.2	0.7	-0.8	-11.0
2019	HOU	15727	-3.5	5.8	-0.5	1.9
2020	TEX	17672	-13.2	2.8	-0.9	-11.2

No one would blame you if you didn't pay particularly close attention to the season Chirinos just had. But 30 games in, he looked like the steal of the off-season as he was was fourth on the Astros in DRC+ with a .278/.412/.567 slash line. For the rest of the season though he hit Extremely Not That. Still, he played 100+ games behind the plate for the second straight season. While he's not a standout framer, he was the second-best blocker in the game behind Roberto Pérez last year, a crucial skill for a team as breaking-ball heavy as Houston. As he enters his age-36 season, he'll look to get a few more one-year deals before riding off into the sunset, presumably after stopping a spiked curveball with a runner on third.

YEAR	TEAM	LVL	AGE	PA	DRC+	VORP	BABIP	BRR	FRAA	WARP
2017	TEX	MLB	33	309	121	20.7	.298	-1.7	C(85): -0.2	2.2
2018	TEX	MLB	34	426	107	21.7	.304	-1.4	C(108): -10.8	1.2
2019	HOU	MLB	35	437	100	23.3	.306	-0.1	C(112): 3.0	2.6
2020	TEX	MLB	36	350	90	4.4	.271	-0.7	C -6	0.0

Robinson Chirinos, continued

Batted Ball Distribution

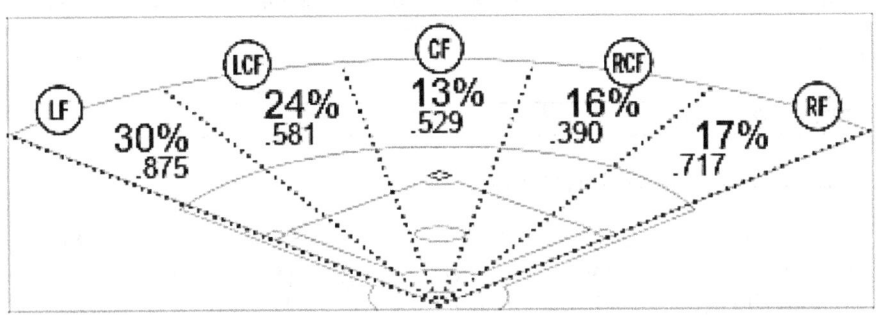

Strike Zone vs LHP   **Strike Zone vs RHP**

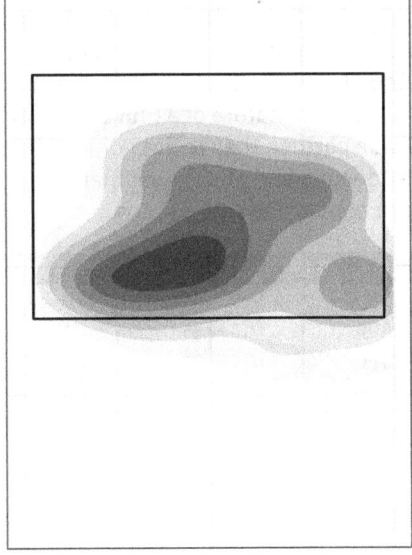

Shin-Soo Choo OF

Born: 07/13/82 Age: 37 Bats: L Throws: L
Height: 5'11" Weight: 210 Origin: International Free Agent, 2000

YEAR	TEAM	LVL	AGE	PA	R	2B	3B	HR	RBI	BB	K	SB	CS	AVG/OBP/SLG
2017	TEX	MLB	34	636	96	20	1	22	78	77	134	12	3	.261/.357/.423
2018	TEX	MLB	35	665	83	30	1	21	62	92	156	6	1	.264/.377/.434
2019	TEX	MLB	36	660	93	31	2	24	61	78	165	15	1	.265/.371/.455
2020	TEX	MLB	37	560	68	24	1	19	69	64	147	7	3	.253/.355/.426

Comparables: Manny Ramirez, Reggie Sanders, Andre Ethier

This is perhaps the most remarkable statistic to come from the Rangers' 2019 season: Choo had 138 plate appearances leading off games for Texas. Here are his numbers in those plate appearances: .345/.449/.621 (1.070) with seven home runs. As Texas begins gearing up for contention with their newly turned-over roster, you'd think those numbers would be enough to get some team interested in Choo. Alas, one gets the sense that potential partners are instead concerned about two other numbers. The first—$21 million, which Choo is due in 2020—is daunting, but could be mitigated slightly by the fact that it's the last year of his contract (and Texas could offer to pay part of it). The other—37, which is the age Choo turned in 2019—has no cure, and will never become less concerning; such is the linear nature of a universe built with no reverse gear. If Texas can't find a trade partner, they're not going to be too upset about it; his clubhouse leadership and easy-going manner are huge assets on a team of guys who are just coming into their prime.

YEAR	TEAM	LVL	AGE	PA	DRC+	VORP	BABIP	BRR	FRAA	WARP
2017	TEX	MLB	34	636	105	11.0	.305	0.7	RF(77): -1.5	1.5
2018	TEX	MLB	35	665	116	25.1	.330	-0.9	RF(34): -2.0, LF(26): -0.6	2.2
2019	TEX	MLB	36	660	113	25.1	.333	-0.2	RF(42): -4.1, LF(40): -0.4	2.0
2020	TEX	MLB	37	560	107	13.4	.325	-0.8	RF -1, LF 0	1.3

Shin-Soo Choo, continued

Batted Ball Distribution

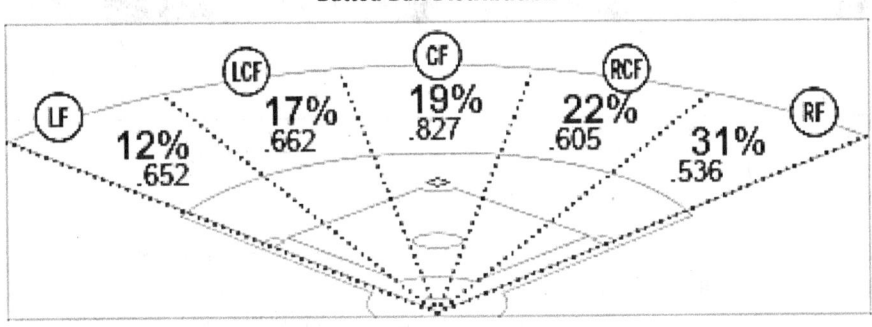

Strike Zone vs LHP

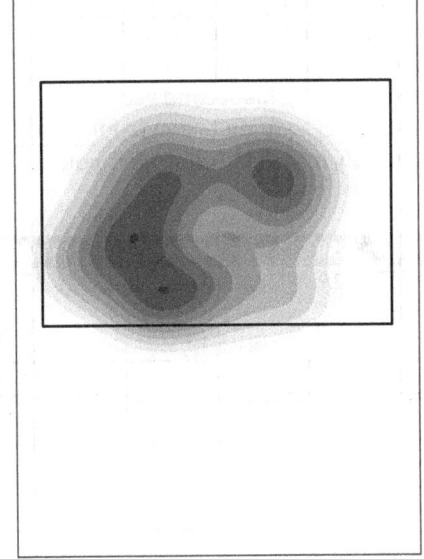

Strike Zone vs RHP

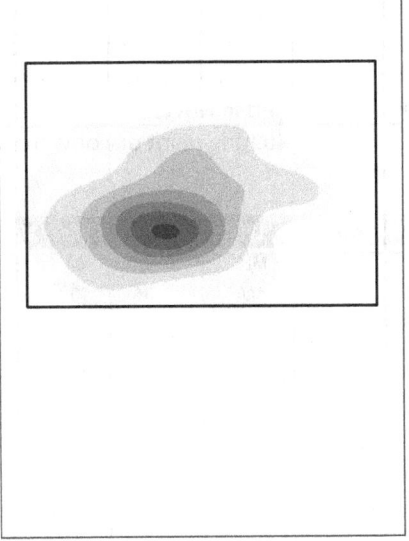

Matt Duffy 3B

Born: 01/15/91 Age: 29 Bats: R Throws: R
Height: 6'2" Weight: 190 Origin: Round 18, 2012 Draft (#568 overall)

YEAR	TEAM	LVL	AGE	PA	R	2B	3B	HR	RBI	BB	K	SB	CS	AVG/OBP/SLG
2018	TBA	MLB	27	560	59	22	1	4	44	47	93	12	6	.294/.361/.366
2019	DUR	AAA	28	36	4	1	0	1	9	1	5	0	0	.273/.306/.394
2019	TBA	MLB	28	169	12	8	0	1	12	19	29	0	1	.252/.343/.327
2020	TBA	MLB	29	251	25	11	1	5	25	20	46	5	2	.258/.325/.376

Comparables: Chris Chambliss, Greg Colbrunn, Terrence Long

Ben Stein's voice personified, Duffy may be the league's least exciting man. He's a pretty good hitter with very little power. He is harmless defender and that is meant in the best way possible. The Rays have primarily played him at third, but he could also play at second, short in a pinch or a corner outfield spot if needed. It is a two-win package, but the problem lies in keeping him on the field long enough to accumulate such production. He has appeared in fewer than 200 games in three and a half seasons with Tampa Bay and did not make his 2019 debut until after the All-Star Break due to back and hamstring maladies. The Rays don't like paying healthy players money, so they really must have hated sending the ACH file with Duffy's direct deposit during his second year of arbitration; and in November they guaranteed they wouldn't have to for a third. If you like watching paint dry or water drip slowly from a faucet, Duff is your man.

YEAR	TEAM	LVL	AGE	PA	DRC+	VORP	BABIP	BRR	FRAA	WARP
2018	TBA	MLB	27	560	104	16.4	.353	-3.9	3B(125): 11.8, SS(1): 0.0	3.1
2019	DUR	AAA	28	36	90	1.7	.286	0.4	3B(5): -0.5, LF(2): -0.1	0.1
2019	TBA	MLB	28	169	88	3.9	.305	-0.3	3B(46): -1.7, SS(1): -0.1	0.2
2020	TBA	MLB	29	251	89	3.6	.305	-0.8	3B 3, SS 0	0.7

Matt Duffy, continued

Batted Ball Distribution

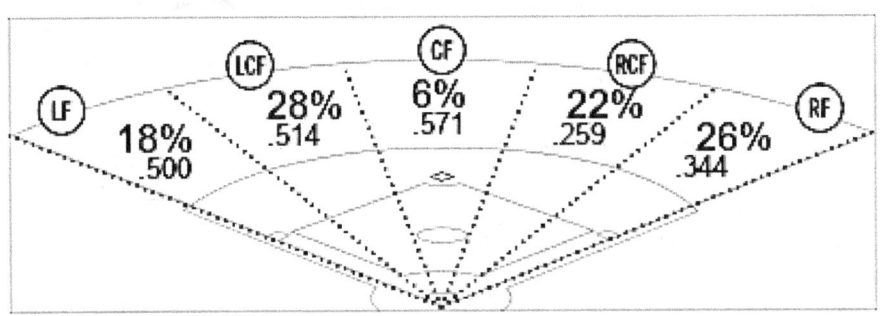

Strike Zone vs LHP **Strike Zone vs RHP**

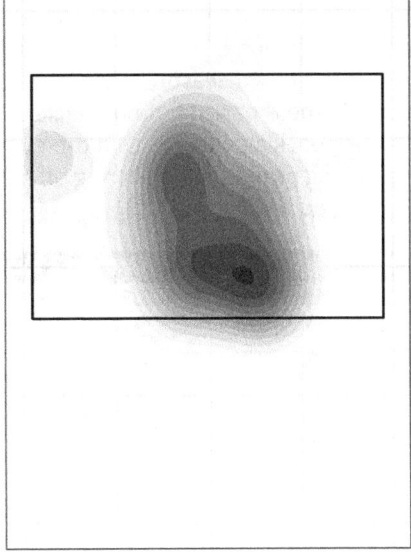

Texas Rangers 2020

Todd Frazier 3B

Born: 02/12/86 Age: 34 Bats: R Throws: R
Height: 6'3" Weight: 220 Origin: Round 1, 2007 Draft (#34 overall)

YEAR	TEAM	LVL	AGE	PA	R	2B	3B	HR	RBI	BB	K	SB	CS	AVG/OBP/SLG
2017	CHA	MLB	31	335	41	15	0	16	44	48	71	4	3	.207/.328/.432
2017	NYA	MLB	31	241	33	4	1	11	32	35	54	0	0	.222/.365/.423
2018	NYN	MLB	32	472	54	18	0	18	59	48	112	9	4	.213/.303/.390
2019	SLU	A+	33	43	3	0	0	1	8	6	8	0	1	.216/.326/.297
2019	NYN	MLB	33	499	63	19	2	21	67	40	106	1	2	.251/.329/.443
2020	NYN	MLB	34	400	47	15	1	17	52	36	94	7	3	.222/.305/.412

Comparables: Josh Donaldson, José Bautista, Troy Glaus

Did you know Frazier is from Toms River, New Jersey? The third baseman, along with Steven Matz, ushered in a brief era where the roster had quite a bit of local flavor. The New York area is not known for producing ballplayers but somehow they all ended up on the Mets last season. Matz and Stroman are of course from Long Island, Rajai Davis hails from Connecticut, Joe Panik the Hudson Valley region, and Brad Brach is from New Jersey—along with Frazier which is certainly news to everyone. True to form, most impending free agents in their mid-30s will spend the offseason fighting back against the system that artificially reduces their market but not Frazier. He spent the first part of the offseason fighting back against the wild turkey population in Toms River, which was damaging property and scaring off residents. You know, since he lives in Toms River. New Jersey.

YEAR	TEAM	LVL	AGE	PA	DRC+	VORP	BABIP	BRR	FRAA	WARP
2017	CHA	MLB	31	335	113	12.5	.214	-0.4	3B(67): 2.2, 1B(4): 0.5	1.9
2017	NYA	MLB	31	241	113	9.9	.244	0.2	3B(66): 1.0	1.4
2018	NYN	MLB	32	472	99	24.3	.241	2.5	3B(109): 5.9	2.5
2019	SLU	A+	33	43	117	0.0	.250	0.1	3B(10): 1.1, 1B(5): -0.1	0.3
2019	NYN	MLB	33	499	104	21.2	.284	0.0	3B(120): 6.5, 1B(3): 0.1	2.7
2020	NYN	MLB	34	400	89	4.9	.251	0.5	3B 2, 1B 0	1.0

Todd Frazier, continued

Batted Ball Distribution

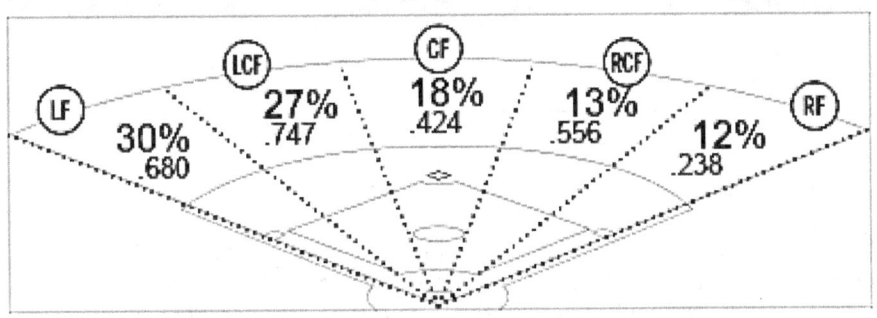

Strike Zone vs LHP   **Strike Zone vs RHP**

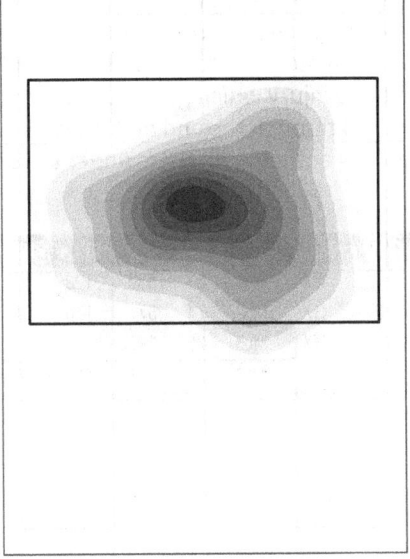

Joey Gallo OF

Born: 11/19/93 Age: 26 Bats: L Throws: R
Height: 6'5" Weight: 235 Origin: Round 1, 2012 Draft (#39 overall)

YEAR	TEAM	LVL	AGE	PA	R	2B	3B	HR	RBI	BB	K	SB	CS	AVG/OBP/SLG
2017	TEX	MLB	23	532	85	18	3	41	80	75	196	7	2	.209/.333/.537
2018	TEX	MLB	24	577	82	24	1	40	92	74	207	3	4	.206/.312/.498
2019	TEX	MLB	25	297	54	15	1	22	49	52	114	4	2	.253/.389/.598
2020	TEX	MLB	26	595	89	27	2	40	103	90	228	5	2	.227/.350/.533

Comparables: Giancarlo Stanton, Dave Nicholson, Reggie Jackson

When Gallo went down with an oblique injury on June 1st, he was hitting .276/.421/.653 (1.074) with 17 home runs and whispers about an MVP candidacy were beginning to circulate around the league. It was the sort of breakout season that the Rangers had hoped was in there somewhere, and if there is one thing that should give Rangers fans hope for the future, it's what Gallo did in April and May. It's always been known that his power could play on Mercury, but the newly added ability to hit to the opposite field, find gaps for extra bases, and manage pitches on the inside corner of the plate are the sorts of additions that turn a fighter jet into a spaceship. Don't bother looking at his statistics after the oblique injury which gave way to a broken hamate bone that kept him out from July 24 through the end of the season. Those are not pretty and we do not enjoy looking at them. Put them under the sheet of shame and pretend they don't exist.

YEAR	TEAM	LVL	AGE	PA	DRC+	VORP	BABIP	BRR	FRAA	WARP
2017	TEX	MLB	23	532	123	27.6	.250	0.5	3B(72): -1.8, 1B(59): 0.5	3.1
2018	TEX	MLB	24	577	116	20.3	.249	1.9	LF(85): -6.3, 1B(35): 3.1	2.7
2019	TEX	MLB	25	297	128	20.3	.368	1.7	CF(38): 0.8, LF(34): 4.1	2.6
2020	TEX	MLB	26	595	126	35.6	.316	1.8	RF 4, CF 0	4.1

Joey Gallo, *continued*

Batted Ball Distribution

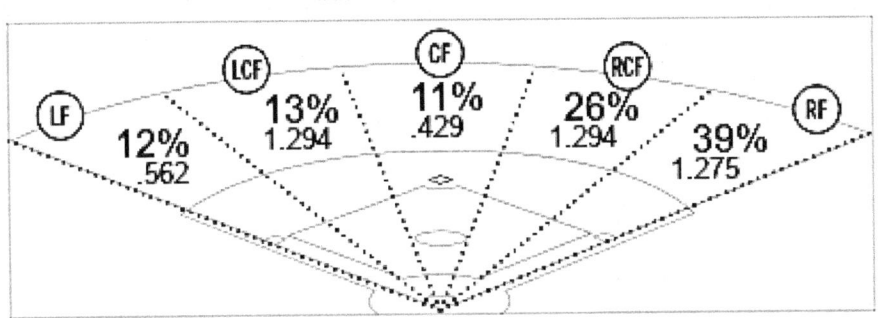

Strike Zone vs LHP   **Strike Zone vs RHP**

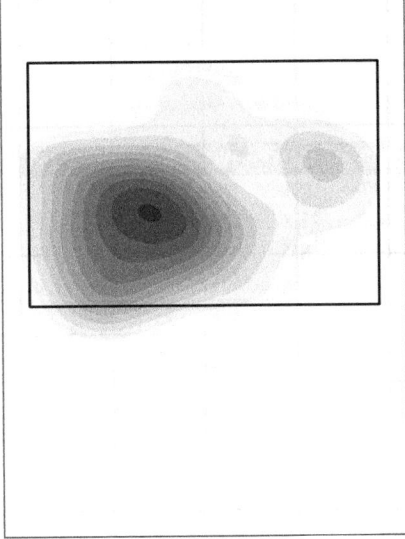

Ronald Guzmán 1B

Born: 10/20/94 Age: 25 Bats: L Throws: L
Height: 6'5" Weight: 225 Origin: International Free Agent, 2011

YEAR	TEAM	LVL	AGE	PA	R	2B	3B	HR	RBI	BB	K	SB	CS	AVG/OBP/SLG
2017	ROU	AAA	22	527	78	22	3	12	62	47	85	4	1	.298/.372/.434
2018	TEX	MLB	23	428	46	18	2	16	58	33	121	1	0	.235/.306/.416
2019	NAS	AAA	24	135	22	8	0	5	16	17	31	0	0	.308/.400/.504
2019	TEX	MLB	24	295	34	20	0	10	36	32	87	1	2	.219/.308/.414
2020	TEX	MLB	25	560	62	25	2	22	72	48	164	1	0	.234/.306/.422

Comparables: Dominic Smith, Rowdy Tellez, Steve Bilko

For all the mathematics involved in analyzing the sport, there's one major difference between math and baseball: When a problem is solved in math, it tends to stay solved. In baseball, all solutions are temporary. Such cat-herding of solutions is the case with first base in Texas, where it appeared after the 2018 season that Guzmán had the position locked up long-term with his exceptional defense and a bat that showed promise of improvement. By the middle of 2019, however, Guzmán was back in Triple-A Nashville, his bat a black hole in the lineup. He hit over .300 upon return to the big leagues, seemingly cured of the mechanical plague that had beset him, so the problem appears to be solved. Again. For now.

YEAR	TEAM	LVL	AGE	PA	DRC+	VORP	BABIP	BRR	FRAA	WARP
2017	ROU	AAA	22	527	115	20.8	.342	-0.3	1B(118): -1.6	1.5
2018	TEX	MLB	23	428	92	2.6	.299	1.9	1B(117): 1.9	0.6
2019	NAS	AAA	24	135	113	6.1	.383	-1.3	1B(22): 0.5	0.3
2019	TEX	MLB	24	295	85	-1.0	.282	-2.5	1B(81): 6.2	0.3
2020	TEX	MLB	25	560	87	0.8	.301	0.0	1B 4	0.5

Ronald Guzmán, continued

Batted Ball Distribution

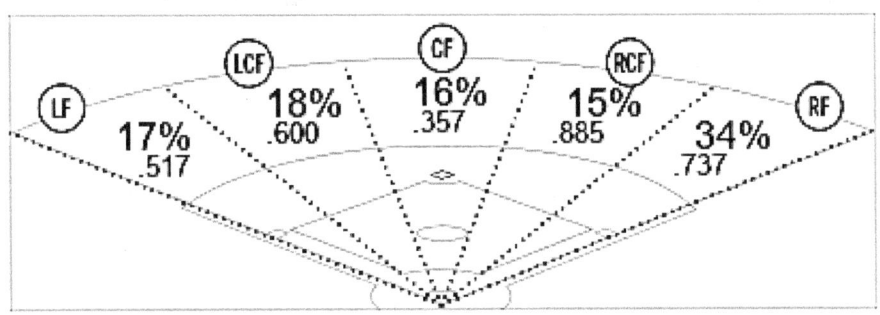

Strike Zone vs LHP   **Strike Zone vs RHP**

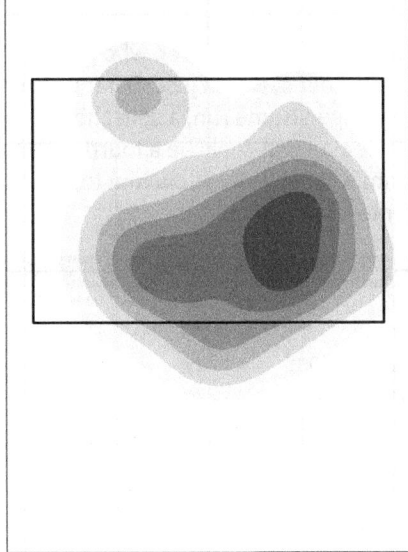

Scott Heineman OF

Born: 12/04/92 Age: 27 Bats: R Throws: R
Height: 6'1" Weight: 215 Origin: Round 11, 2015 Draft (#318 overall)

YEAR	TEAM	LVL	AGE	PA	R	2B	3B	HR	RBI	BB	K	SB	CS	AVG/OBP/SLG
2017	FRI	AA	24	529	82	26	7	9	44	50	121	12	9	.284/.363/.427
2018	FRI	AA	25	31	6	2	0	1	10	7	5	2	1	.522/.613/.739
2018	ROU	AAA	25	469	68	20	2	11	57	32	93	16	8	.295/.355/.429
2019	NAS	AAA	26	182	34	6	2	8	25	17	45	4	3	.340/.412/.553
2019	TEX	MLB	26	85	8	6	0	2	7	9	20	1	2	.213/.306/.373
2020	TEX	MLB	27	280	32	11	2	9	34	21	74	7	3	.252/.321/.422

Comparables: Lorenzo Cain, Sócrates Brito, Matthew den Dekker

When the Rangers' crowded outfield seemed like it was going to block Heineman from a call-up, the team pulled a quick one and started having him play first base in Triple-A. The switch worked—he made his debut on August 2, logging a couple of hits in his first game, however he only ended up playing four games at first base in the big leagues, playing the remainder of his games in the outfield. Scott was the first "Heineman" in big-league history, narrowly edging out his big brother Tyler, who got his first big-league call-up with the Marlins on September 4, which just so happened to also be the night that Scott hit his first big-league home run, a solo shot in Yankee Stadium off Jonathan Loaisiga. Heineman will likely be a fourth outfielder with the Rangers in 2020, though the team will certainly allow him to provide competition for Delino DeShields in center field.

YEAR	TEAM	LVL	AGE	PA	DRC+	VORP	BABIP	BRR	FRAA	WARP
2017	FRI	AA	24	529	114	30.6	.365	6.8	LF(72): -8.5, CF(29): -2.9	1.3
2018	FRI	AA	25	31	270	5.3	.611	-0.9	CF(5): -0.9, LF(2): 0.0	0.4
2018	ROU	AAA	25	469	111	24.6	.353	4.0	RF(48): 1.7, CF(44): -3.3	2.1
2019	NAS	AAA	26	182	139	14.9	.426	-1.1	RF(13): 0.8, LF(11): 1.6	1.3
2019	TEX	MLB	26	85	87	1.0	.264	-0.5	CF(9): -0.5, RF(8): -0.5	-0.1
2020	TEX	MLB	27	280	92	3.6	.320	0.0	LF -1, 1B -1	0.2

Scott Heineman, continued

Batted Ball Distribution

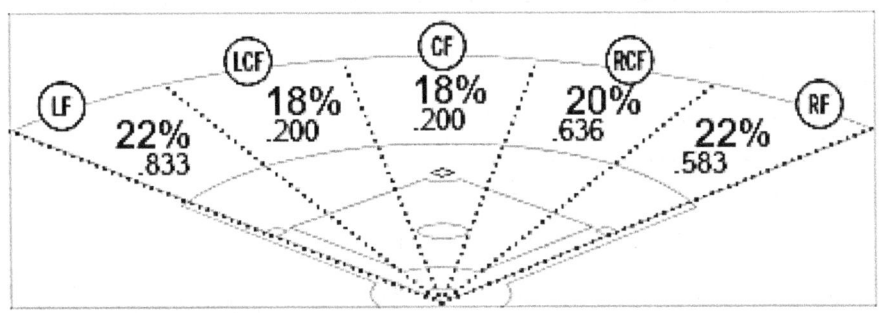

| | Strike Zone vs LHP | Strike Zone vs RHP |

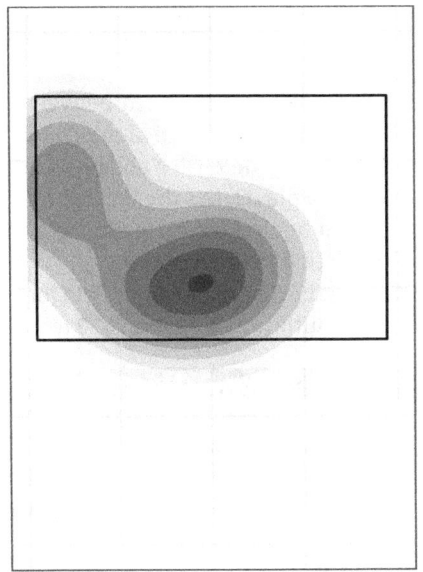
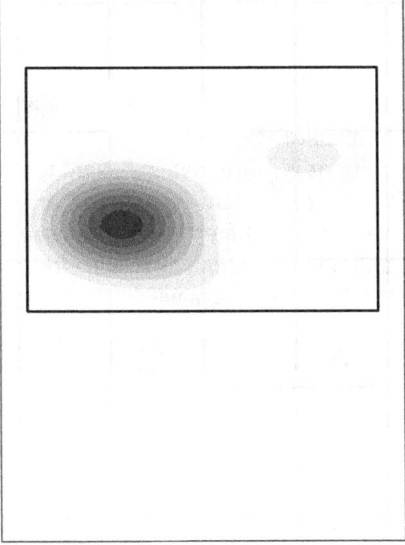

Isiah Kiner-Falefa   UT

Born: 03/23/95   Age: 25   Bats: R   Throws: R
Height: 5'10"   Weight: 176   Origin: Round 4, 2013 Draft (#130 overall)

YEAR	TEAM	LVL	AGE	PA	R	2B	3B	HR	RBI	BB	K	SB	CS	AVG/OBP/SLG
2017	FRI	AA	22	570	58	31	3	5	48	41	72	17	6	.288/.350/.390
2018	TEX	MLB	23	396	43	18	2	4	34	28	62	7	5	.261/.325/.357
2019	FRI	AA	24	71	7	4	0	2	11	8	9	1	0	.283/.380/.450
2019	NAS	AAA	24	37	3	3	0	0	2	1	6	1	0	.147/.216/.235
2019	TEX	MLB	24	222	23	12	1	1	21	14	49	3	0	.238/.299/.322
2020	TEX	MLB	25	280	25	14	1	4	25	19	55	3	2	.247/.313/.351

Comparables: Marwin Gonzalez, Didi Gregorius, Jean Segura

YEAR	TEAM	P. COUNT	FRM RUNS	BLK RUNS	THRW RUNS	TOT RUNS
2017	FRI	4556	-1.1	-0.8	0.0	-1.7
2018	TEX	4896	-9.9	-1.0	0.0	-10.9
2019	FRI	1232	-0.8	0.0	0.0	-0.8
2019	TEX	5069	-9.1	-3.0	0.0	-12.3

There's super-utility, and then there's "No, he can even play catcher." In 2019, the Rangers tried to make Kiner-Falefa exclusively a catcher under the tutelage of Jeff Mathis. After a minor injury, that plan was abandoned. When he began his rehab assignment, he was back to playing around the infield. He's stuck in a bit of an in-between situation: his bat plays well enough for a catcher, but his defense didn't come along quite as quickly as the team hoped. His versatile defensive ability at other positions is more than sufficient to be an everyday player, but the bat has thus far not been potent enough to start anywhere but behind the plate. Round and round it goes. Kiner-Falefa's fate seems uniquely tied to that of Danny Santana—if Santana does win either the starting third base or center field jobs in 2020, Kiner-Falefa will likely slot into the super-utility role on the 2020 team.

YEAR	TEAM	LVL	AGE	PA	DRC+	VORP	BABIP	BRR	FRAA	WARP
2017	FRI	AA	22	570	121	36.8	.325	0.2	3B(50): 6.4, 2B(37): 4.2	4.4
2018	TEX	MLB	23	396	86	3.8	.306	-0.6	3B(46): 3.4, C(35): -10.1	0.1
2019	FRI	AA	24	71	152	6.9	.300	-0.1	C(9): -0.7, 3B(4): 1.5	0.7
2019	NAS	AAA	24	37	34	-4.1	.179	-0.7	SS(4): 0.2, C(2): 0.0	-0.2
2019	TEX	MLB	24	222	72	2.1	.307	1.8	C(38): -11.0, 3B(25): 1.7	-0.5
2020	TEX	MLB	25	280	76	-1.1	.302	0.4	3B 7, 2B 0	0.6

Isiah Kiner-Falefa, continued

Batted Ball Distribution

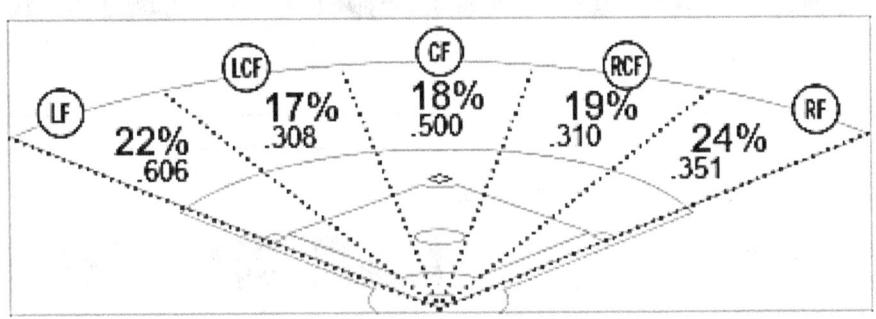

Strike Zone vs LHP **Strike Zone vs RHP**

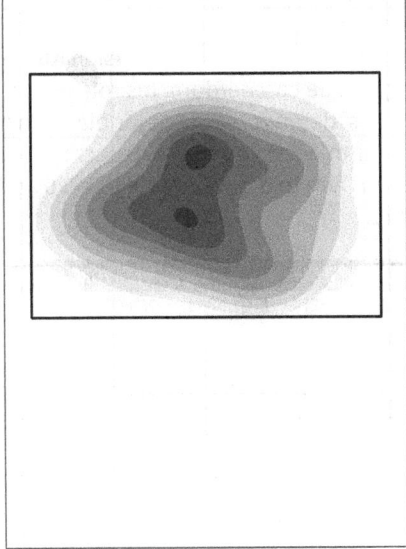

Jeff Mathis C

Born: 03/31/83   Age: 37   Bats: R   Throws: R
Height: 6'0"   Weight: 205   Origin: Round 1, 2001 Draft (#33 overall)

YEAR	TEAM	LVL	AGE	PA	R	2B	3B	HR	RBI	BB	K	SB	CS	AVG/OBP/SLG
2017	ARI	MLB	34	203	13	10	2	2	11	14	61	1	0	.215/.277/.323
2018	ARI	MLB	35	218	15	9	1	1	20	20	66	0	0	.200/.272/.272
2019	TEX	MLB	36	244	17	9	0	2	12	15	87	1	0	.158/.209/.224
2020	TEX	MLB	37	315	24	12	1	5	27	20	111	1	0	.191/.247/.292

Comparables: Jason LaRue, Kelly Stinnett, Nick Hundley

YEAR	TEAM	P. COUNT	FRM RUNS	BLK RUNS	THRW RUNS	TOT RUNS
2017	ARI	7723	8.9	-0.7	1.1	8.9
2018	ARI	8583	11.8	2.3	0.0	14.1
2019	TEX	11104	-1.8	0.8	-1.0	-2.1
2020	TEX	8129	4.7	0.4	-0.5	4.6

It raised some eyebrows when the Rangers let Robinson Chirinos walk in free agency before the 2019 season, and those same eyebrows kept creeping toward the nearest hairline when Texas decided to replace Chirinos by signing Mathis to a two-year deal. After all, Mathis was a career backup—he hadn't caught more than 70 games since 2013. But with Isiah Kiner-Falefa and Jose Trevino on the verge of big-league catcherdom, his role would be something resembling player-coach. Mathis' defense was a major player in the decision, but his hitting was probably closer to what you might expect from a coach. Texas will almost undoubtedly return him to a backup role in 2020 as Trevino transitions into a more full-time role.

YEAR	TEAM	LVL	AGE	PA	DRC+	VORP	BABIP	BRR	FRAA	WARP
2017	ARI	MLB	34	203	59	-1.5	.309	0.4	C(58): 10.2	1.0
2018	ARI	MLB	35	218	63	-3.3	.292	-0.4	C(63): 18.5, 2B(1): -0.1	2.0
2019	TEX	MLB	36	244	41	-5.9	.243	0.7	C(86): -2.8, P(2): 0.0	-0.8
2020	TEX	MLB	37	315	40	-10.0	.288	0.2	C 10	0.0

Jeff Mathis, continued

Batted Ball Distribution

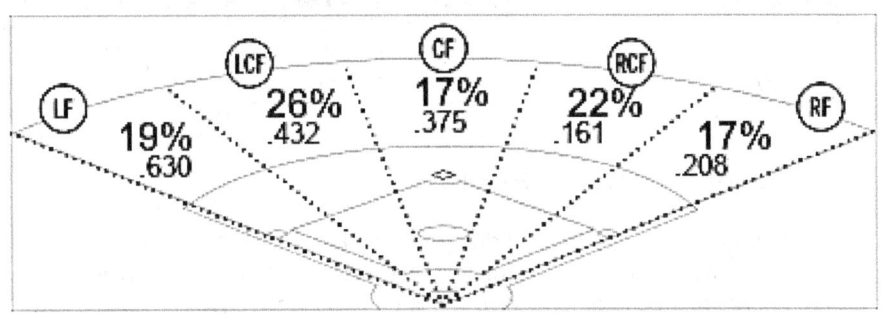

Strike Zone vs LHP   Strike Zone vs RHP

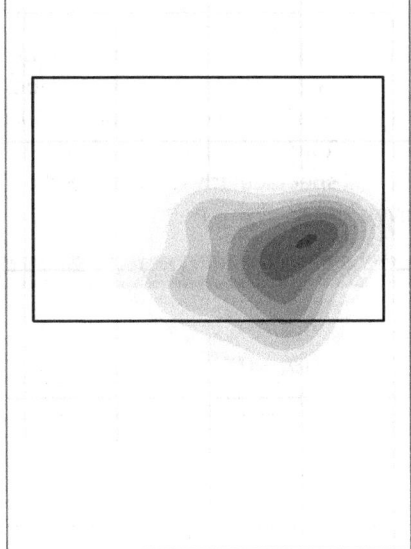

Rangers Player Analysis - 41

Rougned Odor   2B

Born: 02/03/94   Age: 26   Bats: L   Throws: R
Height: 5'11"   Weight: 195   Origin: International Free Agent, 2011

YEAR	TEAM	LVL	AGE	PA	R	2B	3B	HR	RBI	BB	K	SB	CS	AVG/OBP/SLG
2017	TEX	MLB	23	651	79	21	3	30	75	32	162	15	6	.204/.252/.397
2018	TEX	MLB	24	535	76	23	2	18	63	43	127	12	12	.253/.326/.424
2019	TEX	MLB	25	581	77	30	1	30	93	52	178	11	9	.205/.283/.439
2020	TEX	MLB	26	595	70	26	3	30	84	39	170	11	6	.222/.283/.443

Comparables: Addison Russell, Jurickson Profar, Wilmer Flores

You put your finger on the page, didn't you? You put your index finger on the page and scrolled down, looking for this very name so that you could feel the potent energy of anger coursing through your veins. It's a powerful feeling, the superiority that comes from knowing more than a so-called expert. "I can't believe the media keeps buying this same old story," you think, shaking your head. "He's had hot streaks before. This won't last. It never lasts. He doesn't care. He's a problem. He needs to shave his beard and button up his shirt," you mutter, satisfied that if only the world would heed your advice, everything would make more sense. You're right, of course. It would make more sense, to you—maybe even to a sizable number of people. To this we say: you might be right! You should go apply for the GM job. Also, we have no idea what kind of player Rougned Odor is going to be in 2020, beyond this one small prediction: he will spectacularly either exceed or fall short of projections. But seriously, who even knows at this point?

YEAR	TEAM	LVL	AGE	PA	DRC+	VORP	BABIP	BRR	FRAA	WARP
2017	TEX	MLB	23	651	75	-9.7	.224	1.3	2B(158): 6.2	0.7
2018	TEX	MLB	24	535	97	14.5	.305	1.0	2B(127): 7.5	2.4
2019	TEX	MLB	25	581	87	9.3	.244	-2.8	2B(137): -12.8	-0.6
2020	TEX	MLB	26	595	84	11.2	.264	0.4	2B 0	1.1

Rougned Odor, continued

Batted Ball Distribution

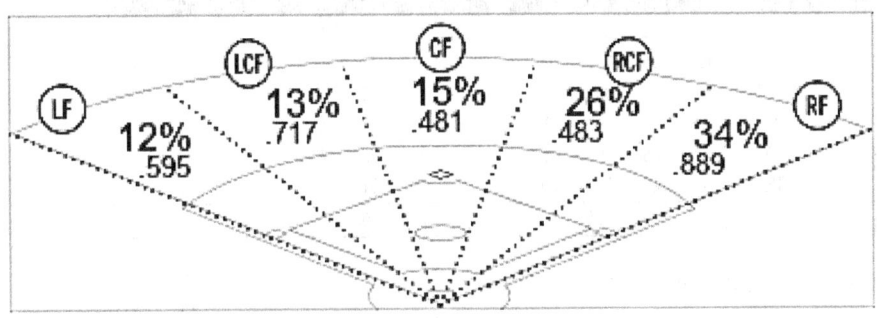

Strike Zone vs LHP   **Strike Zone vs RHP**

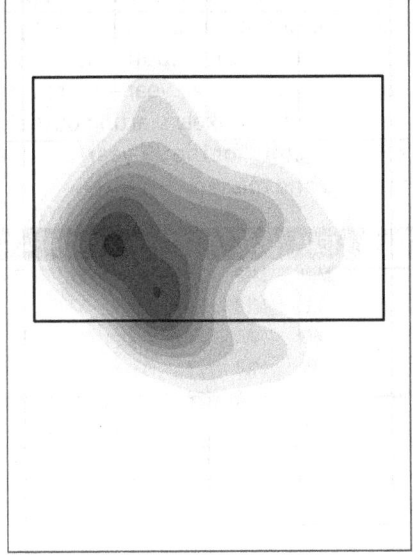

Texas Rangers 2020

Danny Santana CF

Born: 11/07/90 Age: 29 Bats: B Throws: R
Height: 5'11" Weight: 185 Origin: International Free Agent, 2007

YEAR	TEAM	LVL	AGE	PA	R	2B	3B	HR	RBI	BB	K	SB	CS	AVG/OBP/SLG
2017	MIN	MLB	26	26	3	1	0	1	1	1	8	1	0	.200/.231/.360
2017	ATL	MLB	26	152	16	9	2	3	22	7	33	6	0	.203/.245/.357
2018	GWN	AAA	27	342	57	21	3	16	40	15	80	12	5	.264/.294/.497
2018	ATL	MLB	27	32	4	3	0	0	2	3	11	1	1	.179/.281/.286
2019	NAS	AAA	28	40	4	4	1	0	6	4	10	1	1	.343/.425/.514
2019	TEX	MLB	28	511	81	23	6	28	81	25	151	21	6	.283/.324/.534
2020	TEX	MLB	29	595	68	26	6	25	80	28	176	20	8	.248/.289/.450

Comparables: Jacque Jones, Austin Jackson, Ender Inciarte

Santana had a breakout year in 2019 after signing a minor-league deal with the Rangers, finally living up to the high expectations he set for himself after a great rookie campaign preceded years of fumbled opportunities. So impressive was the performance that the Rangers opted to keep him in the system rather than take advantage of the buy low/sell high situation at the trade deadline. In the end, a full turn into adapting that fly-ball lifestyle—which he started in Atlanta and Gwinnett the prior year—led to him more than tripling his major-league home run total. A likely starting outfield job awaits Santana in 2020 and that in itself is a victory for the 29-year-old, even if it all comes crumbling down in a fit of swings and misses.

YEAR	TEAM	LVL	AGE	PA	DRC+	VORP	BABIP	BRR	FRAA	WARP
2017	MIN	MLB	26	26	59	-1.2	.250	0.2	LF(8): 0.8, RF(3): 0.0	0.0
2017	ATL	MLB	26	152	62	-0.8	.243	2.0	LF(30): 2.7, 2B(7): -0.6	0.1
2018	GWN	AAA	27	342	105	14.4	.301	1.5	CF(45): 1.1, 2B(14): 1.3	1.8
2018	ATL	MLB	27	32	71	-1.0	.294	-0.7	LF(6): 0.1, CF(3): -0.1	-0.1
2019	NAS	AAA	28	40	117	4.8	.480	1.1	RF(3): -0.2, SS(3): 0.8	0.3
2019	TEX	MLB	28	511	106	18.0	.353	3.6	1B(44): 0.9, CF(27): 0.6	2.1
2020	TEX	MLB	29	595	87	10.5	.315	1.6	CF -1, 1B 0	1.2

Danny Santana, continued

Batted Ball Distribution

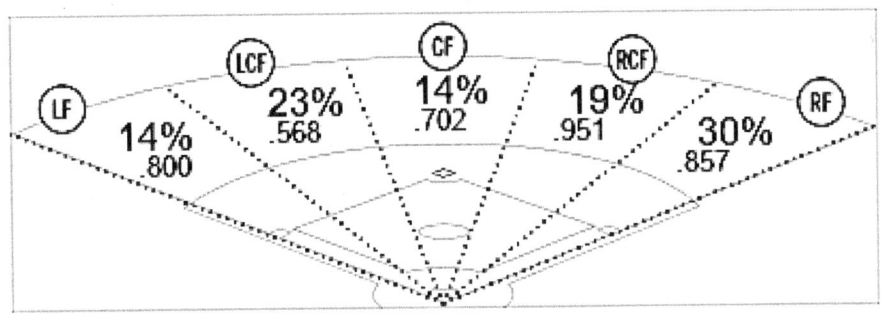

Strike Zone vs LHP **Strike Zone vs RHP**

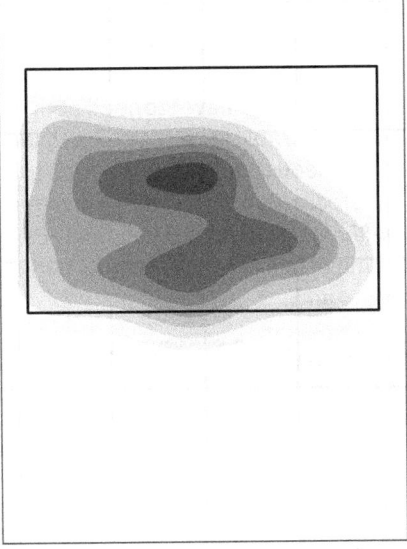

Nick Solak 2B

Born: 01/11/95 Age: 25 Bats: R Throws: R
Height: 5'11" Weight: 190 Origin: Round 2, 2016 Draft (#62 overall)

YEAR	TEAM	LVL	AGE	PA	R	2B	3B	HR	RBI	BB	K	SB	CS	AVG/OBP/SLG
2017	TAM	A+	22	406	56	17	4	10	44	53	76	13	4	.301/.397/.460
2017	TRN	AA	22	132	16	9	1	2	9	10	24	1	1	.286/.344/.429
2018	MNT	AA	23	565	91	17	3	19	76	68	112	21	6	.282/.384/.450
2019	DUR	AAA	24	349	56	13	1	17	47	39	80	3	2	.266/.353/.485
2019	NAS	AAA	24	128	23	6	0	10	27	6	25	2	0	.347/.386/.653
2019	TEX	MLB	24	135	19	6	1	5	17	15	29	2	0	.293/.393/.491
2020	TEX	MLB	25	560	70	23	2	25	78	47	135	7	2	.267/.340/.469

Comparables: Preston Tucker, Brandon Lowe, Logan Forsythe

When the Rangers traded Pete Fairbanks to the Tampa Bay Rays for Solak, the assessment was clear: the kid was going to hit, and he was going to work extremely hard. Shifting the conversation to defense, however, elicited a high-pitched and uncertain groan from scouts—the sort of sound when your car is telling you that you have 22 miles to empty and you're 22.5 miles from the nearest gas station and your spouse asks if you're going to make it. *"Ehhhhhhhhh,"* you reply in an upper register. *"Ehhhhhhhh,"* because "It's a coin flip and I should have stopped at the last place" is too frank an admission, and "Yeah, no problem" sets you up to look like a fool. So you say *"Ehhhhhhh,"* simultaneously admitting that it's touch and go while also indicating that you don't really want to talk too much more about it. Can Solak play second base? *Ehhhhhh…* Third base? Left field? *Ehhhhhhh…* Solak will no doubt enter 2020 hoping to answer those doubts and change the first letter of that answer from an E to an S.

YEAR	TEAM	LVL	AGE	PA	DRC+	VORP	BABIP	BRR	FRAA	WARP
2017	TAM	A+	22	406	173	39.3	.357	2.5	2B(92): 1.4	4.0
2017	TRN	AA	22	132	108	8.1	.340	0.5	2B(30): 2.0	0.8
2018	MNT	AA	23	565	141	46.4	.330	-0.5	2B(61): -6.9, LF(40): -3.3	2.9
2019	DUR	AAA	24	349	108	10.3	.303	-3.6	2B(61): -7.5, LF(17): 0.4	0.3
2019	NAS	AAA	24	128	135	14.6	.369	0.7	2B(21): 0.4, RF(4): 0.3	1.0
2019	TEX	MLB	24	135	109	5.1	.354	1.3	3B(11): -0.1, 2B(5): -0.7	0.6
2020	TEX	MLB	25	560	110	20.1	.319	-0.2	3B -4, 2B 0	1.6

Nick Solak, continued

Batted Ball Distribution

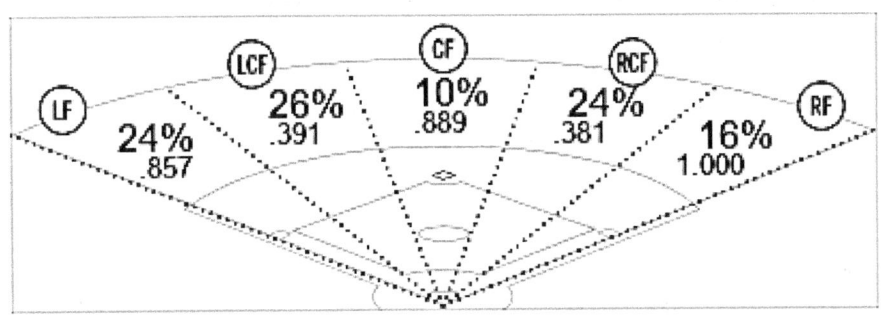

Strike Zone vs LHP   **Strike Zone vs RHP**

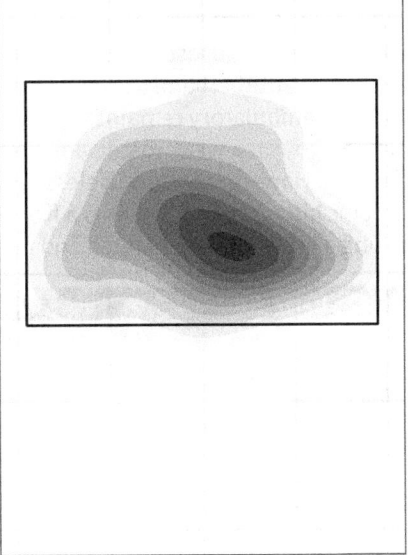

Texas Rangers 2020

Sam Travis OF/1B
Born: 08/27/93 Age: 26 Bats: R Throws: R
Height: 6'0" Weight: 205 Origin: Round 2, 2014 Draft (#67 overall)

YEAR	TEAM	LVL	AGE	PA	R	2B	3B	HR	RBI	BB	K	SB	CS	AVG/OBP/SLG
2017	PAW	AAA	23	342	40	14	0	6	24	37	57	6	2	.270/.351/.375
2017	BOS	MLB	23	83	13	6	0	1	6	6	23	1	0	.263/.325/.342
2018	PAW	AAA	24	398	35	13	0	8	43	29	89	1	2	.258/.317/.360
2018	BOS	MLB	24	38	5	3	0	1	7	2	10	0	0	.222/.263/.389
2019	PAW	AAA	25	268	36	14	1	7	33	31	62	5	1	.275/.362/.432
2019	BOS	MLB	25	157	17	4	1	6	16	11	36	2	0	.215/.274/.382
2020	BOS	MLB	26	35	3	2	0	1	4	3	8	0	0	.231/.299/.369

Comparables: Brandon Snyder, Nick Evans, Chris Marrero

It wasn't supposed to be the hit tool. Travis was never projected to hit for power, and he's never been known for his glove. But the hit tool was supposed to be safe. Well, he's got nearly 300 major-league plate appearances under his belt now and that small but not insignificant sample tells us Travis kinda stinks. There were 49 first basemen who recorded as many plate appearances as the 2014 draft pick did last season and among them he ranked 40th in DRC+, ahead of Cheslor Cuthbert and Justin Bour, to his eternal credit, but also behind Neil Walker's ambulatory remains. Travis's ceiling at this point is as the short-side platoon guy on a weak roster, and he should *never* be allowed to face same-side pitching. Honestly, he's so useless against righties it's a wonder Nancy Pelosi isn't his hitting coach. Travis is a fine organizational depth piece, but if you're seeing a lot of him after March and before September, something's gone wrong.

YEAR	TEAM	LVL	AGE	PA	DRC+	VORP	BABIP	BRR	FRAA	WARP
2017	PAW	AAA	23	342	117	-0.1	.315	-3.5	1B(58): -0.1	0.6
2017	BOS	MLB	23	83	68	-3.8	.377	-1.0	1B(21): 0.2	-0.3
2018	PAW	AAA	24	398	94	9.1	.317	1.3	1B(45): 0.5, LF(36): -2.7	0.3
2018	BOS	MLB	24	38	80	-0.4	.280	0.0	LF(6): 0.0, 1B(3): -0.1	0.0
2019	PAW	AAA	25	268	114	11.8	.347	-0.3	LF(31): -2.3, 1B(26): -0.1	0.6
2019	BOS	MLB	25	157	83	-0.2	.243	-0.1	1B(29): 0.1, LF(18): 0.5	0.0
2020	BOS	MLB	26	35	78	-0.5	.288	-0.1	1B 0	-0.1

Sam Travis, continued

Batted Ball Distribution

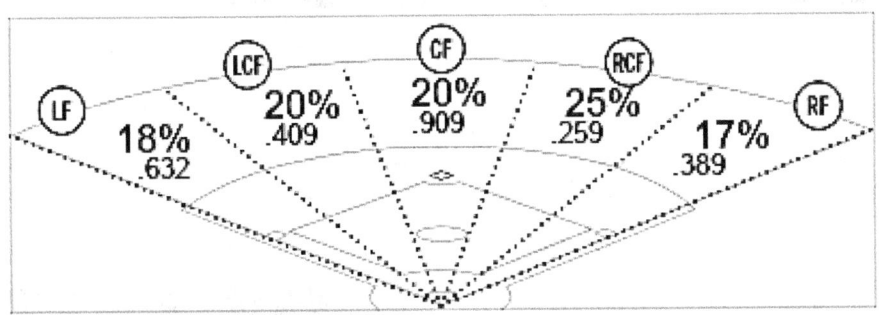

Strike Zone vs LHP   **Strike Zone vs RHP**

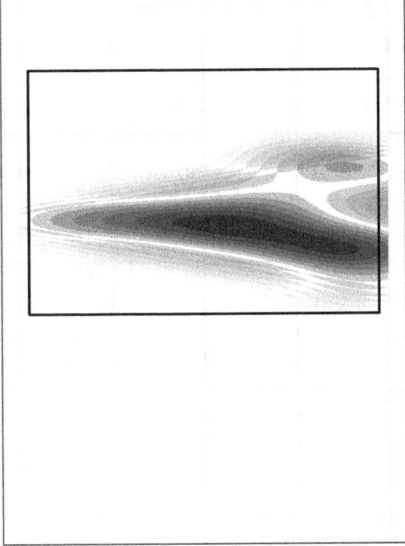

Jose Trevino C

Born: 11/28/92 Age: 27 Bats: R Throws: R
Height: 5'11" Weight: 211 Origin: Round 6, 2014 Draft (#186 overall)

YEAR	TEAM	LVL	AGE	PA	R	2B	3B	HR	RBI	BB	K	SB	CS	AVG/OBP/SLG
2017	FRI	AA	24	423	39	12	0	7	42	19	44	1	2	.241/.275/.323
2018	FRI	AA	25	201	18	7	1	3	16	13	27	0	1	.234/.284/.332
2018	TEX	MLB	25	8	0	0	0	0	3	0	1	0	0	.250/.250/.250
2019	NAS	AAA	26	156	16	10	0	2	22	8	28	2	0	.226/.263/.336
2019	TEX	MLB	26	126	18	9	0	2	13	3	27	0	0	.258/.272/.383
2020	TEX	MLB	27	315	27	15	0	8	32	13	63	0	0	.231/.266/.359

Comparables: Alberto Rosario, Bruce Maxwell, Gustavo Molina

YEAR	TEAM	P. COUNT	FRM RUNS	BLK RUNS	THRW RUNS	TOT RUNS
2017	FRI	13448	24.9	4.7	0.5	30.2
2018	FRI	5456	6.0	0.5	0.6	6.7
2018	TEX	277	-0.2	-0.2	0.0	-0.6
2019	NAS	5534	7.3	0.2	0.0	7.0
2019	TEX	5125	0.8	0.0	0.0	0.6
2020	TEX	2682	0.5	0.0	0.1	0.5

A multiple minor-league Gold Glove winner and extraordinary clubhouse presence, Trevino's bat has always been the big question. By August of 2019, Trevino was in the big leagues and given a legitimate shot at proving he could stick. Before a rough final couple of weeks, the 26-year-old was hitting .282 with the Rangers. The next glaring deficiency is going to be selectivity at the plate—in 76 September plate appearances, Trevino worked just two walks (up from just one in 48 August PAs). According to the fine folks at Brooks Baseball, that's a result of two things: pitchers being very willing to throw him fastballs and changeups in the strike zone, and his willingness to swing at breaking pitches that are not in the zone. He should get another legitimate shot to show improvement at the plate in 2020, though Sam Huff's ascendant surge through the minor leagues could signal an ultimate fate for Trevino that resembles another defense-first catcher: career backup Jeff Mathis.

YEAR	TEAM	LVL	AGE	PA	DRC+	VORP	BABIP	BRR	FRAA	WARP
2017	FRI	AA	24	423	66	-0.3	.256	-0.1	C(99): 32.1	4.0
2018	FRI	AA	25	201	73	-0.7	.255	-0.8	C(38): 8.0	1.1
2018	TEX	MLB	25	8	82	-0.6	.286	0.0	C(3): -0.5	0.0
2019	NAS	AAA	26	156	46	-3.1	.263	0.7	C(40): 6.4	0.5
2019	TEX	MLB	26	126	77	2.9	.312	-0.7	C(40): 0.5	0.3
2020	TEX	MLB	27	315	61	-1.9	.269	-0.7	C 3	0.1

Jose Trevino, continued

Batted Ball Distribution

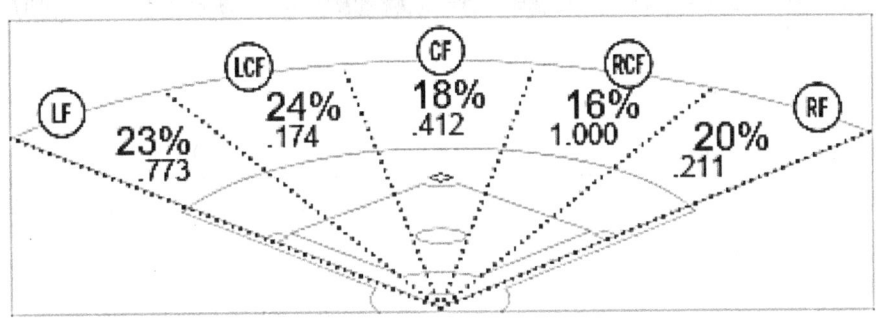

Strike Zone vs LHP   **Strike Zone vs RHP**

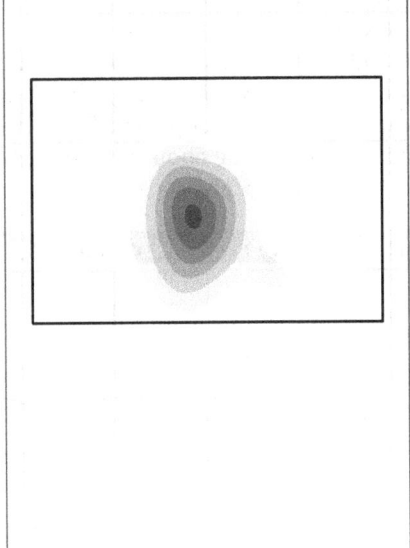

Kolby Allard LHP

Born: 08/13/97   Age: 22   Bats: L   Throws: L
Height: 6'1"   Weight: 190   Origin: Round 1, 2015 Draft (#14 overall)

YEAR	TEAM	LVL	AGE	W	L	SV	G	GS	IP	H	HR	BB/9	K/9	K	GB%	BABIP
2017	MIS	AA	19	8	11	0	27	27	150	146	11	2.7	7.7	129	44%	.310
2018	GWN	AAA	20	6	4	0	19	19	112^1	102	6	2.7	7.1	89	39%	.296
2018	ATL	MLB	20	1	1	0	3	1	8	19	3	4.5	3.4	3	36%	.444
2019	GWN	AAA	21	7	5	0	20	20	110	119	15	2.9	8.0	98	51%	.331
2019	TEX	MLB	21	4	2	0	9	9	45^1	52	3	3.8	6.6	33	46%	.327
2020	TEX	MLB	22	3	3	0	10	10	51	60	9	3.3	6.0	34	46%	.312

Comparables: Julio Teheran, Taijuan Walker, Mike Soroka

When Allard was 18, the Braves watched him breeze through rookie ball and A-Ball. At 19, he made quick work of Double-A opponents. Then in 2018, still just 20 and shrugging off Triple-A hitters, he was called up to the big leagues and that… did not go well. When he looked hittable at Triple-A Gwinnett at 21 in 2019, Atlanta traded him to the Rangers for relief pitcher Chris Martin. After Allard posted a sparkling 0.00 ERA in Nashville for, um, one game, the Rangers brought him up. It wasn't a dominant two months—he didn't strike many hitters out, and he walked too many—but Allard showed the ability to keep a cool head when waters got choppy. The Rangers won six and lost three with Allard on the mound. He'll battle about a half-dozen other young starters for a spot on the 25-man roster in 2020.

YEAR	TEAM	LVL	AGE	WHIP	ERA	DRA	WARP	MPH	FB%	WHF	CSP
2017	MIS	AA	19	1.27	3.18	4.72	0.8				
2018	GWN	AAA	20	1.21	2.72	4.34	1.5				
2018	ATL	MLB	20	2.88	12.38	8.43	-0.3	91.1	62.7	5.6	46.5
2019	GWN	AAA	21	1.41	4.17	4.53	2.3				
2019	TEX	MLB	21	1.57	4.96	6.04	-0.1	93.7	46.4	8.6	52.5
2020	TEX	MLB	22	1.54	5.65	5.28	0.2	93.4	50.6	8.5	51.9

Kolby Allard, continued

Pitch Shape vs LHH

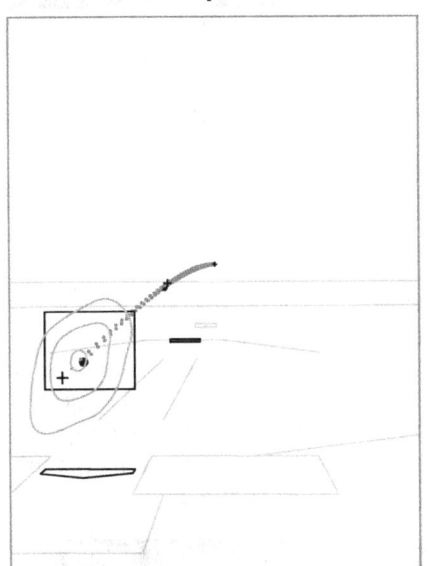

Pitch Shape vs RHH

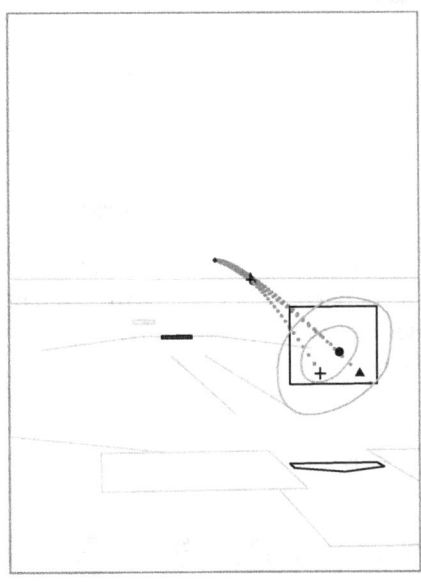

Type	Frequency	Velocity	H Movement	V Movement
● Fastball	46.4%	92.5 [100]	8.1 [95]	-15.1 [102]
☐ Sinker				
+ Cutter	33.2%	87.8 [94]	-2.4 [104]	-26.2 [92]
▲ Changeup	15.1%	81.7 [87]	11.9 [96]	-28 [98]
✕ Splitter				
▽ Slider				
◇ Curveball	5.4%	77.6 [97]	-3.8 [85]	-47.8 [100]
✦ Slow Curveball				
✹ Knuckleball				
▼ Screwball				

Cody Allen RHP

Born: 11/20/88 Age: 31 Bats: R Throws: R
Height: 6'1" Weight: 210 Origin: Round 23, 2011 Draft (#698 overall)

YEAR	TEAM	LVL	AGE	W	L	SV	G	GS	IP	H	HR	BB/9	K/9	K	GB%	BABIP
2017	CLE	MLB	28	3	7	30	69	0	67[1]	57	9	2.8	12.3	92	34%	.304
2018	CLE	MLB	29	4	6	27	70	0	67	58	11	4.4	10.7	80	31%	.292
2019	ROC	AAA	30	0	2	0	7	1	8	7	1	5.6	7.9	7	27%	.286
2019	LAA	MLB	30	0	2	4	25	0	23	24	9	7.8	11.3	29	20%	.263
2020	MIN	MLB	31	2	2	0	33	0	35	31	7	4.3	10.6	41	30%	.279

Comparables: Troy Percival, Francisco Rodríguez, Ugueth Urbina

Allen lost about a mile-and-a-half per hour off his heater from 2018 to 2019. Some pitchers can survive that kind of velocity loss by relying on their secondaries and de-emphasizing the importance of the fastball in their repertoire. Allen isn't that kind of guy, as his once simple-but-effective two-pitch arsenal left little room to manuever. Hitters knew they could sit on the curveball and still catch up to his defanged fastball, leading Allen to nibble, leading to an increased walk rate. Add all that to a 65 percent fly ball rate amidst the year of the rocket ball, and you get the season Cody Allen just endured.

YEAR	TEAM	LVL	AGE	WHIP	ERA	DRA	WARP	MPH	FB%	WHF	CSP
2017	CLE	MLB	28	1.16	2.94	2.64	1.9	95.8	55.5	15.5	41.8
2018	CLE	MLB	29	1.36	4.70	3.61	1.0	95.3	60.3	13.9	43.1
2019	ROC	AAA	30	1.50	3.38	6.50	0.0				
2019	LAA	MLB	30	1.91	6.26	8.94	-0.9	94.3	53.7	10.6	41.8
2020	MIN	MLB	31	1.35	4.79	4.71	0.2	94.4	56.8	13.6	42

Cody Allen, continued

Pitch Shape vs LHH

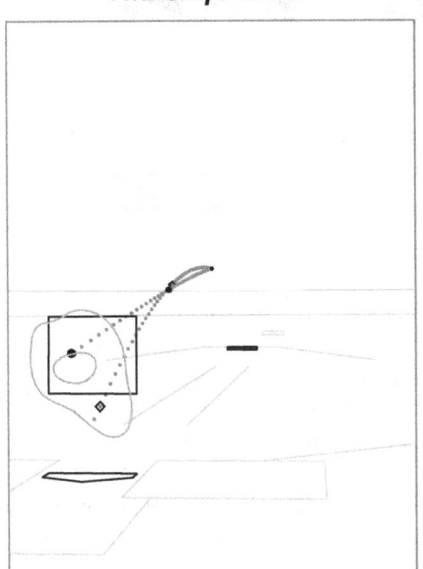

Pitch Shape vs RHH

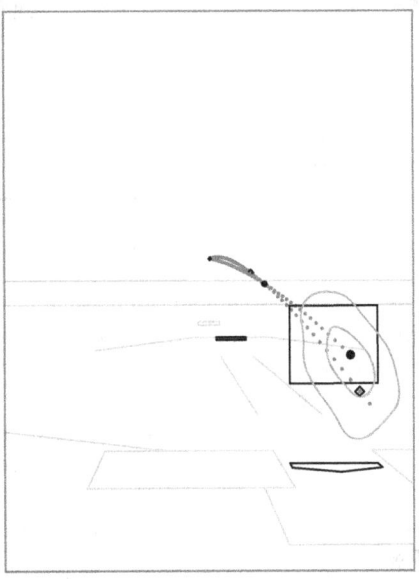

Type	Frequency	Velocity	H Movement	V Movement
● Fastball	53.7%	92.9 [102]	-9 [90]	-12.2 [110]
☐ Sinker				
+ Cutter				
▲ Changeup				
× Splitter				
▽ Slider				
◇ Curveball	46.3%	83.3 [115]	8.2 [103]	-42.2 [111]
⬥ Slow Curveball				
✻ Knuckleball				
▼ Screwball				

Kyle Bird LHP

Born: 04/12/93   Age: 27   Bats: L   Throws: L
Height: 6'2"   Weight: 175   Origin: Round 35, 2014 Draft (#1057 overall)

YEAR	TEAM	LVL	AGE	W	L	SV	G	GS	IP	H	HR	BB/9	K/9	K	GB%	BABIP
2017	MNT	AA	24	4	2	0	53	0	71^1	64	2	3.7	8.6	68	46%	.316
2018	MNT	AA	25	0	2	4	16	1	19^2	14	2	4.1	10.5	23	43%	.267
2018	DUR	AAA	25	3	1	0	27	5	55^2	38	4	4.2	10.5	65	40%	.264
2019	NAS	AAA	26	5	1	2	29	0	34^2	35	4	3.9	10.1	39	42%	.344
2019	TEX	MLB	26	0	0	1	12	0	12^2	11	5	10.7	7.1	10	42%	.182
2020	TEX	MLB	27	2	2	0	31	0	33	33	6	4.4	7.2	26	40%	.277

Comparables: Buddy Baumann, Williams Jerez, Scott Alexander

There's an old saying about Nashville, that it's a "five-year town." The implication is that with so many musicians coming and going from their hometowns in hopes of making it big, it takes about five years before the locals will begin to trust that you're going to stick around—finally accepting you as one of them. After Kyle Bird's 2019 season, expect that number to go up. He spent five separate stints in Music City between big-league call-ups. Bird's performance in the bright lights of Nashville suggested that he was ready for the big stage, but—as many a country musician can tell you—if it doesn't play in Texas, it's not quite good enough yet.

YEAR	TEAM	LVL	AGE	WHIP	ERA	DRA	WARP	MPH	FB%	WHF	CSP
2017	MNT	AA	24	1.30	3.03	4.55	0.2				
2018	MNT	AA	25	1.17	3.66	3.82	0.3				
2018	DUR	AAA	25	1.15	1.94	3.15	1.3				
2019	NAS	AAA	26	1.44	2.86	4.33	0.6				
2019	TEX	MLB	26	2.05	7.82	7.33	-0.3	93.4	53.3	10	46.5
2020	TEX	MLB	27	1.49	5.50	5.21	0.0	92.9	54	10.1	47.1

Kyle Bird, continued

Pitch Shape vs LHH

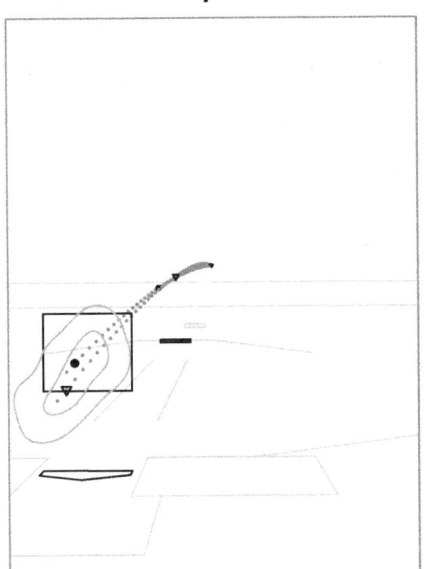

Pitch Shape vs RHH

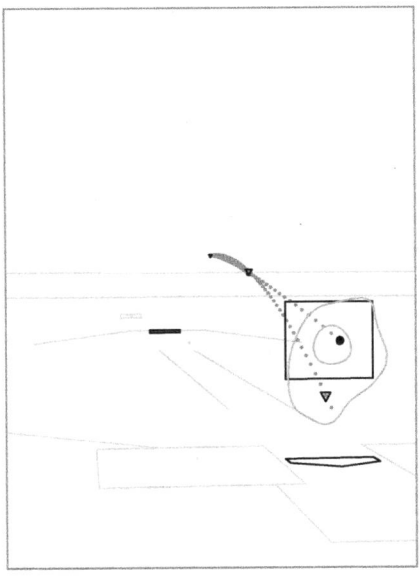

Type	Frequency	Velocity	H Movement	V Movement
● Fastball	49.2%	91.6 [98]	8.6 [92]	-18.7 [93]
□ Sinker	4.2%	90.3 [88]	12 [104]	-23.6 [89]
+ Cutter				
▲ Changeup				
✕ Splitter				
▽ Slider	46.3%	80 [81]	-9.9 [120]	-39.7 [81]
◇ Curveball				
✦ Slow Curveball				
✱ Knuckleball				
▼ Screwball				

Brock Burke LHP

Born: 08/04/96 Age: 23 Bats: L Throws: L
Height: 6'4" Weight: 180 Origin: Round 3, 2014 Draft (#96 overall)

YEAR	TEAM	LVL	AGE	W	L	SV	G	GS	IP	H	HR	BB/9	K/9	K	GB%	BABIP
2017	BGR	A	20	6	0	0	10	10	57^1	37	0	3.1	9.3	59	35%	.253
2017	PCH	A+	20	5	6	0	13	13	66	75	6	2.2	6.7	49	47%	.329
2018	PCH	A+	21	3	5	0	16	13	82	85	4	3.3	9.5	87	48%	.343
2018	MNT	AA	21	6	1	0	9	9	55^1	39	2	2.3	11.5	71	37%	.282
2019	FRI	AA	22	3	5	0	9	9	45^1	34	2	2.4	9.7	49	50%	.262
2019	NAS	AAA	22	0	0	0	2	2	8	12	1	6.8	12.4	11	50%	.478
2019	TEX	MLB	22	0	2	0	6	6	26^2	30	6	3.7	4.7	14	52%	.276
2020	TEX	MLB	23	1	2	0	5	5	22	26	4	3.3	4.8	12	46%	.296

Comparables: Stephen Gonsalves, Robbie Ray, Lucas Sims

When Burke was first called up, his manager joked that the young left-hander was so unbothered by the big lights and pressure of the big leagues that it seemed like he was up there yawning between pitches. That statement became a bit more loaded when it came out that Burke had dealt with somnambulism (sleep walking) since childhood. Of all the young Rangers starters to make their big-league debuts in 2019, Burke might have the highest ceiling. He looked magnificent in his first couple of starts, but an illness and shoulder fatigue led to some performances that made his end-of-season stats look a bit bloated. Neither issue is expected to require anything more than rest over the offseason, and the Rangers hope that Burke will earn a rotation spot in spring training.

YEAR	TEAM	LVL	AGE	WHIP	ERA	DRA	WARP	MPH	FB%	WHF	CSP
2017	BGR	A	20	0.99	1.10	2.69	1.7				
2017	PCH	A+	20	1.38	4.64	5.46	-0.2				
2018	PCH	A+	21	1.40	3.84	4.77	0.5				
2018	MNT	AA	21	0.96	1.95	2.91	1.6				
2019	FRI	AA	22	1.01	3.18	2.73	1.2				
2019	NAS	AAA	22	2.25	7.88	6.74	0.0				
2019	TEX	MLB	22	1.54	7.43	6.82	-0.3	94.3	61.3	5.7	51
2020	TEX	MLB	23	1.56	6.07	5.65	0.0	94.2	63.5	5.9	52.8

Brock Burke, continued

Pitch Shape vs LHH

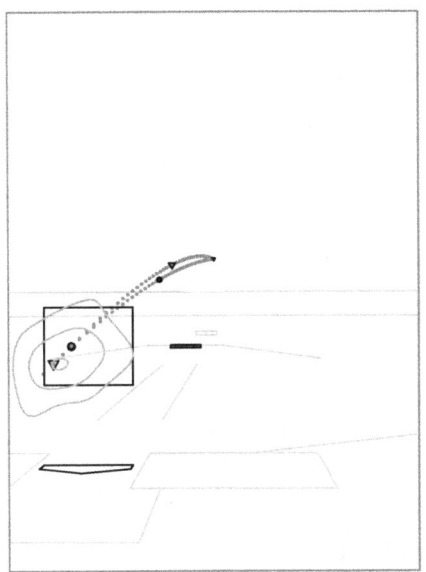

Pitch Shape vs RHH

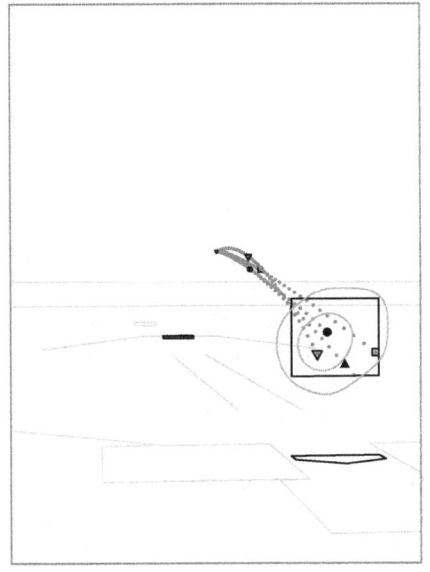

Type	Frequency	Velocity	H Movement	V Movement
● Fastball	43.9%	92.3 [100]	7.1 [99]	-15.5 [101]
□ Sinker	17.4%	91.1 [92]	13.7 [93]	-22 [94]
+ Cutter				
▲ Changeup	16.0%	85.6 [101]	9.8 [106]	-28.4 [97]
✕ Splitter				
▽ Slider	22.7%	80.6 [84]	-6.5 [106]	-37.9 [86]
◇ Curveball				
⊕ Slow Curveball				
✱ Knuckleball				
▼ Screwball				

Jesse Chavez   RHP

Born: 08/21/83   Age: 36   Bats: R   Throws: R
Height: 6'2"   Weight: 175   Origin: Round 42, 2002 Draft (#1252 overall)

YEAR	TEAM	LVL	AGE	W	L	SV	G	GS	IP	H	HR	BB/9	K/9	K	GB%	BABIP
2017	LAA	MLB	33	7	11	0	38	21	138	148	28	2.9	7.8	119	42%	.306
2018	TEX	MLB	34	3	1	1	30	0	56¹	58	10	1.9	8.0	50	45%	.296
2018	CHN	MLB	34	2	1	4	32	0	39	26	3	1.2	9.7	42	43%	.247
2019	TEX	MLB	35	3	5	1	48	9	78	82	12	2.5	8.3	72	42%	.310
2020	TEX	MLB	36	2	2	4	47	0	49	55	11	2.8	8.2	45	42%	.304

Comparables: Jay Howell, Dan Wheeler, Bob Howry

Fun with stats: Chavez as an opener in 2019: 4 games, 6 2/3 innings, 0 earned runs, 0 walks, 7 strikeouts. Chavez as a starter in 2019: 5 games, 23 1/3 innings, 20 earned runs (7.71 ERA), 5 walks, 21 strikeouts. Of course, there's context needed: Chavez "opened" against the Astros, Mariners, Mariners, and Reds, and started against the Tigers (0 ER), Rays (3 ER), Twins (4 ER), Astros (6 ER), and Diamondbacks (7 ER). Whether the decline in results came from the back-and-forth is the sort of thing that leads to speculation, as is the question of whether stretching him out led to the injuries that spiked the end of his season (surgery to remove loose bodies from his elbow). Side note: The best Chavez story of the season takes place on July 12. After home plate umpire Rob Drake had blown two ball/strike calls in the hitters' favor, Chavez exaggeratedly offered his prescription sunglasses to Drake as he walked off the field. After the game, he did not back down from the display. "I thought he needed 'em," Chavez shrugged.

YEAR	TEAM	LVL	AGE	WHIP	ERA	DRA	WARP	MPH	FB%	WHF	CSP
2017	LAA	MLB	33	1.40	5.35	4.80	1.1	93.5	61	9.2	46
2018	TEX	MLB	34	1.24	3.51	3.20	1.1	94.7	92.9	11.7	53.6
2018	CHN	MLB	34	0.79	1.15	2.95	0.9	94.5	92.9	11.5	53
2019	TEX	MLB	35	1.33	4.85	5.07	0.4	92.8	70.8	7.8	48
2020	TEX	MLB	36	1.42	5.50	5.28	0.0	92.3	72.5	9.3	48.2

Jesse Chavez, continued

Pitch Shape vs LHH

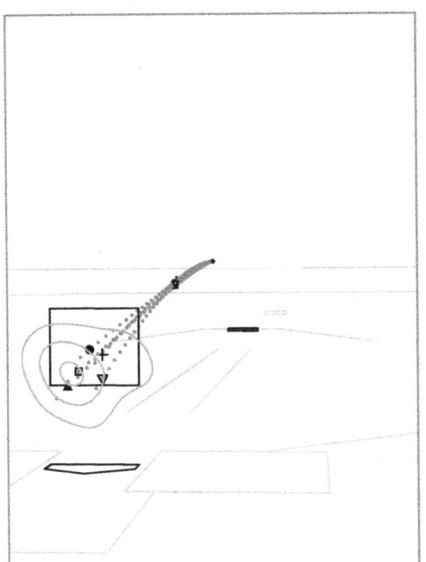

Pitch Shape vs RHH

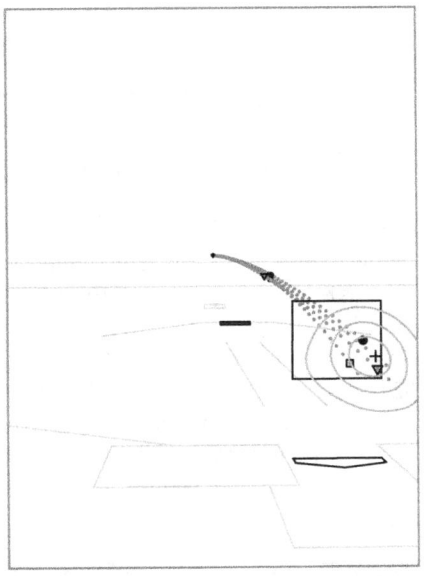

Type	Frequency	Velocity	H Movement	V Movement
● Fastball	6.4%	91.8 [98]	-9.1 [90]	-15.4 [101]
□ Sinker	38.4%	91.4 [93]	-15.2 [83]	-21.9 [95]
+ Cutter	26.0%	88.9 [101]	-0.7 [85]	-20.1 [115]
▲ Changeup	9.4%	85.4 [101]	-15.8 [78]	-30 [92]
✕ Splitter				
▽ Slider	19.6%	86.9 [110]	3.4 [93]	-25.6 [122]
◇ Curveball				
✦ Slow Curveball				
✱ Knuckleball				
▼ Screwball				

Luis García RHP

Born: 01/30/87   Age: 33   Bats: R   Throws: R
Height: 6'2"   Weight: 240   Origin: International Free Agent, 2017

YEAR	TEAM	LVL	AGE	W	L	SV	G	GS	IP	H	HR	BB/9	K/9	K	GB%	BABIP
2017	PHI	MLB	30	2	5	2	66	0	71[1]	61	3	3.3	7.6	60	57%	.282
2018	PHI	MLB	31	3	1	1	59	0	46	49	4	3.5	10.0	51	50%	.354
2019	LAA	MLB	32	2	1	1	64	2	62	61	13	4.8	8.3	57	49%	.282
2020	LAA	MLB	33	2	2	0	33	0	35	33	4	4.5	9.2	36	52%	.304

Comparables: Sam Freeman, Blaine Hardy, Cory Gearrin

Current baseball discussions that mention the name "Luis García" are typically followed by a question: "The Phillies one or the Nationals one?" For the Angels, the answer was "neither," as their García is a journeyman reliever rather than a promising teenage shortstop. An up-and-down bullpen arm for the Phillies over several seasons, García spent virtually all of his 2019 in the Angels' 'pen, logging 62 largely forgettable innings. Like many fringy arms, García suffered from the Three True Outcomes tendencies of the game, with his strikeout ability not quite compensating for the plentiful walks and home runs. The Angels did their part to turn the Luis García question into an either/or, releasing theirs following the season.

YEAR	TEAM	LVL	AGE	WHIP	ERA	DRA	WARP	MPH	FB%	WHF	CSP
2017	PHI	MLB	30	1.22	2.65	3.26	1.5	99.0	63.3	12.8	49
2018	PHI	MLB	31	1.46	6.07	3.25	0.9	99.5	48.4	15.5	44.8
2019	LAA	MLB	32	1.52	4.35	5.87	-0.3	99.2	47	13.1	43.6
2020	LAA	MLB	33	1.45	4.52	4.49	0.3	98.1	51.1	13.5	44.8

Luis García, continued

Pitch Shape vs LHH

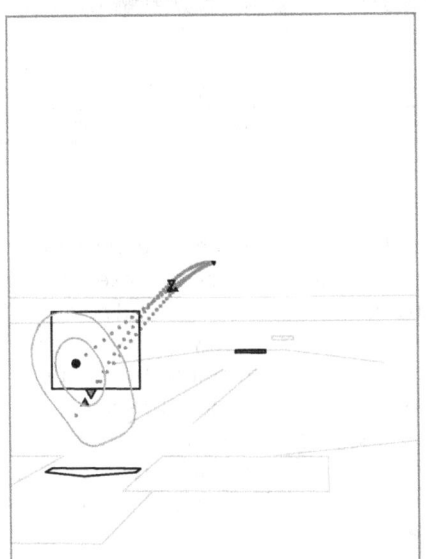

Pitch Shape vs RHH

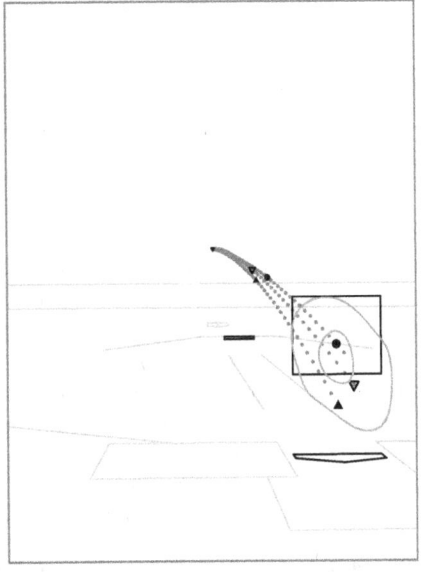

Type	Frequency	Velocity	H Movement	V Movement
● Fastball	45.6%	97.4 [114]	-9.5 [88]	-15.5 [101]
□ Sinker				
+ Cutter				
▲ Changeup	18.6%	87 [106]	-5.4 [127]	-29.4 [94]
✕ Splitter				
▽ Slider	34.4%	85.5 [105]	6.6 [107]	-33.2 [100]
◇ Curveball				
⊕ Slow Curveball				
✻ Knuckleball				
▼ Screwball				

Kyle Gibson RHP

Born: 10/23/87 Age: 32 Bats: R Throws: R
Height: 6'6" Weight: 215 Origin: Round 1, 2009 Draft (#22 overall)

YEAR	TEAM	LVL	AGE	W	L	SV	G	GS	IP	H	HR	BB/9	K/9	K	GB%	BABIP
2017	MIN	MLB	29	12	10	0	29	29	158	182	24	3.4	6.9	121	52%	.328
2018	MIN	MLB	30	10	13	0	32	32	196^2	177	23	3.6	8.2	179	51%	.285
2019	MIN	MLB	31	13	7	0	34	29	160	175	23	3.2	9.0	160	52%	.331
2020	TEX	MLB	32	9	9	0	26	26	150	159	19	3.9	9.0	150	52%	.324

Comparables: Joe Kelly, Brandon McCarthy, Iván Nova

When you have a type, you have a type. Texas pounced on Gibson early in free agency, signing the now-former Twin to a three-year deal that mimicked the deals inked by Mike Minor and Lance Lynn, the club's most successful recent rotation reclamations. The healthy portions of Gibson's past two seasons have looked similar, but last year's final tallies were skewed after ulcerative colitis ripped 15 pounds off his frame and tanked his second half. His four-seamer continues to be highly problematic, but he finally started to get away from the pitch last year, giving in to the good deal of depth in the rest of his repertoire. If he pitches to his potential, he's a good bet to mark a third straight year of successful rotation bargain-binning by the Rangers.

YEAR	TEAM	LVL	AGE	WHIP	ERA	DRA	WARP	MPH	FB%	WHF	CSP
2017	MIN	MLB	29	1.53	5.07	5.20	0.7	94.6	56.7	10.6	42.2
2018	MIN	MLB	30	1.30	3.62	4.21	2.5	95.3	57.8	12.1	40.4
2019	MIN	MLB	31	1.44	4.84	5.60	0.3	95.4	50.3	13	38.5
2020	TEX	MLB	32	1.48	4.87	4.59	1.7	94.2	54.1	12	39.7

Kyle Gibson, continued

Pitch Shape vs LHH

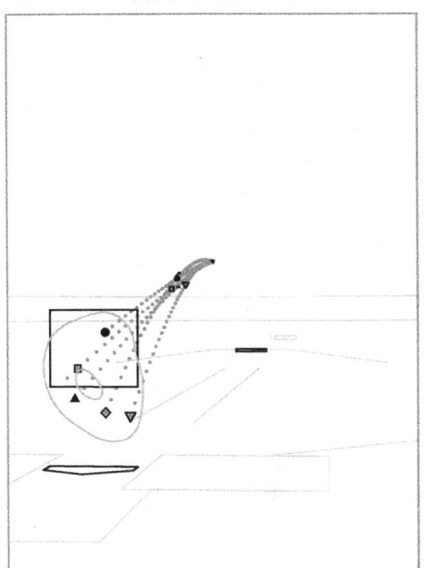

Pitch Shape vs RHH

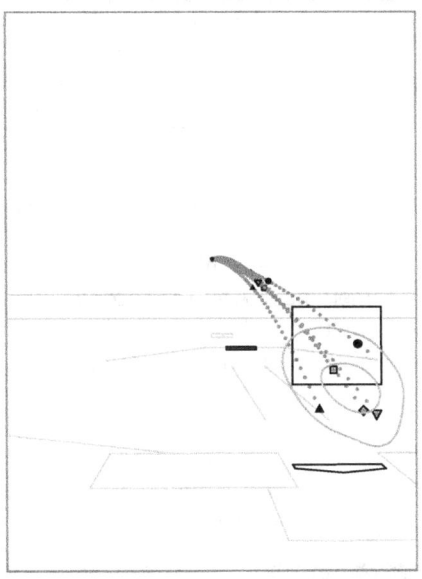

Type	Frequency	Velocity	H Movement	V Movement
● Fastball	17.9%	93.8 [104]	-4.8 [109]	-13.5 [106]
□ Sinker	32.4%	93.6 [105]	-12 [104]	-17.5 [110]
+ Cutter				
▲ Changeup	16.1%	85.7 [102]	-11.7 [97]	-28 [98]
✕ Splitter				
▽ Slider	20.2%	84.4 [100]	5 [100]	-35.5 [93]
◇ Curveball	13.3%	80.6 [107]	6.1 [94]	-45.3 [105]
⊕ Slow Curveball				
✻ Knuckleball				
▼ Screwball				

Nick Goody RHP

Born: 07/06/91 Age: 28 Bats: R Throws: R
Height: 5'11" Weight: 200 Origin: Round 6, 2012 Draft (#217 overall)

YEAR	TEAM	LVL	AGE	W	L	SV	G	GS	IP	H	HR	BB/9	K/9	K	GB%	BABIP
2017	CLE	MLB	25	1	2	0	56	0	54²	39	7	3.3	11.9	72	29%	.269
2018	CLE	MLB	26	0	2	0	12	0	11²	15	4	3.9	9.3	12	30%	.306
2019	COH	AAA	27	0	1	0	21	0	24¹	28	8	4.8	12.6	34	26%	.345
2019	CLE	MLB	27	3	2	0	39	0	40²	30	7	4.9	11.1	50	26%	.245
2020	TEX	MLB	28	2	2	0	41	0	44	36	8	3.5	10.8	53	28%	.263

Comparables: Fernando Cabrera, Edubray Ramos, Dominic Leone

Entering the season's final weekend, Goody had a chance to finish with a 2.something ERA for the second time in three tries. If he was aware of that information, it didn't set well on him. Instead, Goody faced six batters and permitted four of them to reach (all four later scored). His ERA ended up at 3.54—an achievement, considering he'd appeared 39 times and departed with his seasonal ERA at least that high on just four occasions. What a grim, predictable surprise, seeing all that hard work wasted. It must be how the ants feel: always on the precipice of success, or, more often, existential dismay. Goody? No. Not quite.

YEAR	TEAM	LVL	AGE	WHIP	ERA	DRA	WARP	MPH	FB%	WHF	CSP
2017	CLE	MLB	25	1.08	2.80	2.66	1.5	93.4	52.4	17.5	42.5
2018	CLE	MLB	26	1.71	6.94	5.33	-0.1	93.4	54.8	14.4	40.7
2019	COH	AAA	27	1.68	7.77	6.41	0.0				
2019	CLE	MLB	27	1.28	3.54	5.92	-0.3	94.1	51.1	16.4	44.1
2020	TEX	MLB	28	1.20	3.92	3.95	0.6	93.2	52.3	16.7	42.8

Nick Goody, continued

Pitch Shape vs LHH

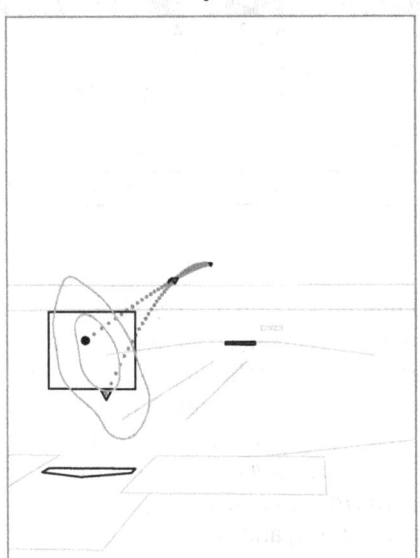

Pitch Shape vs RHH

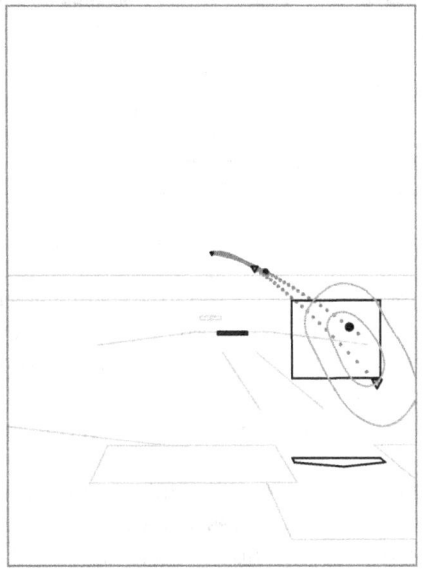

Type	Frequency	Velocity	H Movement	V Movement
● Fastball	51.1%	92.8 [101]	-5.2 [107]	-13.5 [106]
☐ Sinker				
+ Cutter				
▲ Changeup				
✕ Splitter				
▽ Slider	48.9%	82.4 [92]	8.8 [116]	-35.2 [94]
◇ Curveball				
✦ Slow Curveball				
✳ Knuckleball				
▼ Screwball				

Texas Rangers 2020

Ariel Jurado   RHP
Born: 01/30/96   Age: 24   Bats: R   Throws: R
Height: 6'1"   Weight: 180   Origin: International Free Agent, 2002

YEAR	TEAM	LVL	AGE	W	L	SV	G	GS	IP	H	HR	BB/9	K/9	K	GB%	BABIP
2017	FRI	AA	21	9	11	0	27	27	157	188	16	2.1	5.4	95	53%	.335
2018	FRI	AA	22	5	3	0	16	16	101^2	107	12	1.5	5.1	58	51%	.291
2018	TEX	MLB	22	5	5	0	12	8	54^2	66	7	3.0	3.6	22	52%	.304
2019	NAS	AAA	23	3	0	0	4	4	22^2	29	1	0.8	8.7	22	39%	.400
2019	TEX	MLB	23	7	11	0	32	18	122^1	148	21	2.6	6.0	81	48%	.318
2020	TEX	MLB	24	3	4	0	34	8	65	80	11	2.7	5.7	42	47%	.319

Comparables: Zach Eflin, Luis Ortiz, Jake Thompson

Once in awhile it's fun to use a player's comments section to write about something else entirely. This year, it's Jurado who gets the treatment. Today, we're going to highlight one way to know you're dating the wrong person. In any relationship, your significant other will inevitably do things that delight you and things that vex you; that's just how humanity works! We all have the capacity to annoy the &%#$ out of each other, to varying degrees, but the hope is that you eventually find someone who is worth the annoyances, someone who mostly behaves in a way that enhances your joy, and when they do something you don't like, it kind of comes as a surprise. When you're in a relationship with the wrong person, the opposite tends to occur: when they do something that delights you, you find that it comes as a surprise. "That was incredibly sweet," you exclaim, eyebrows furrowing as the entire realization sets in. "But…it was kind of out of character, wasn't it? What on earth does it mean that I'm surprised by them doing something good?" Eventually, if you pull the thread long enough, you'll reach the inevitable conclusion that the kind act was a surprise because it was out of character—a gesture, rather than a reflection of who they are.

And that's how you know.

YEAR	TEAM	LVL	AGE	WHIP	ERA	DRA	WARP	MPH	FB%	WHF	CSP
2017	FRI	AA	21	1.43	4.59	5.64	-0.9				
2018	FRI	AA	22	1.22	3.28	4.40	1.1				
2018	TEX	MLB	22	1.54	5.93	6.97	-1.1	93.7	70.2	4.8	51.2
2019	NAS	AAA	23	1.37	3.57	4.85	0.4				
2019	TEX	MLB	23	1.50	5.81	7.21	-2.0	94.5	64.2	8.3	48.9
2020	TEX	MLB	24	1.52	5.72	5.35	0.1	94.1	67.7	7.6	51.4

Ariel Jurado, continued

Pitch Shape vs LHH

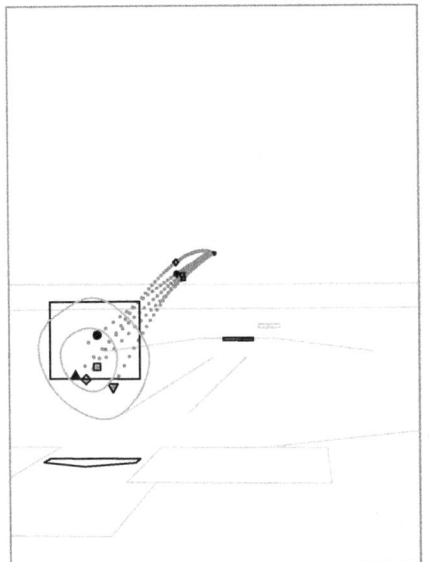

Pitch Shape vs RHH

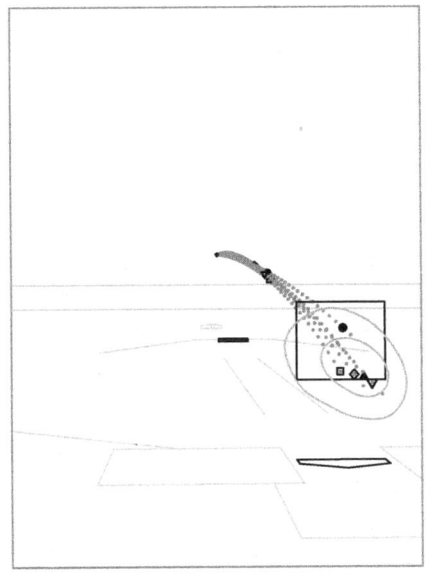

Type	Frequency	Velocity	H Movement	V Movement
● Fastball	22.9%	93.4 [103]	-7.6 [97]	-15 [102]
☐ Sinker	41.3%	92.2 [98]	-14.2 [90]	-22.2 [94]
+ Cutter				
▲ Changeup	11.9%	85.5 [101]	-13.2 [91]	-24.6 [108]
✕ Splitter				
▽ Slider	14.7%	85.5 [105]	1.7 [86]	-32.1 [103]
◇ Curveball	9.3%	80.7 [107]	4.5 [88]	-42 [112]
✦ Slow Curveball				
✱ Knuckleball				
▼ Screwball				

Shawn Kelley RHP

Born: 04/26/84 Age: 36 Bats: R Throws: R
Height: 6'2" Weight: 237 Origin: Round 13, 2007 Draft (#405 overall)

YEAR	TEAM	LVL	AGE	W	L	SV	G	GS	IP	H	HR	BB/9	K/9	K	GB%	BABIP
2017	WAS	MLB	33	3	2	4	33	0	26	29	12	3.8	8.7	25	26%	.236
2018	WAS	MLB	34	1	0	0	35	0	32^1	26	7	1.4	8.9	32	28%	.229
2018	OAK	MLB	34	1	0	0	19	0	16^2	7	0	3.2	9.7	18	40%	.184
2019	TEX	MLB	35	5	2	11	50	0	47^1	55	12	2.1	8.2	43	30%	.314
2020	TEX	MLB	36	2	2	0	33	0	35	33	9	2.3	8.9	35	31%	.262

Comparables: Rafael Soriano, Blake Parker, Darren O'Day

A year ago, Kelley was the guy who power-slammed his glove in Washington and promptly traded to the A's. In Texas, he inherited a new role: closer. His 11 saves were a career high, probably giving the Rangers more value than they expected from the veteran. It wasn't enough to convince them to exercise his 2020 option, however. Kelley said during the season that if that option weren't picked up, he would retire rather than re-enter free agency. One might argue that throwing a still-functioning glove at the ground was some kind of predictive metaphor for this decision, but given the minor injuries he endured in 2019, it's also reasonable to accept that this 35-year-old is just ready to stop hurling things altogether and spend more time with his family.

YEAR	TEAM	LVL	AGE	WHIP	ERA	DRA	WARP	MPH	FB%	WHF	CSP
2017	WAS	MLB	33	1.54	7.27	6.11	-0.3	94.3	59.2	15.4	46.9
2018	WAS	MLB	34	0.96	3.34	4.51	0.2	94.5	52.8	12.4	50.7
2018	OAK	MLB	34	0.78	2.16	3.22	0.3	93.1	50.6	12.4	50.1
2019	TEX	MLB	35	1.39	4.94	6.43	-0.6	94.3	39.7	12.4	49.8
2020	TEX	MLB	36	1.20	4.56	4.78	0.2	92.9	46.6	12.7	48.3

Shawn Kelley, continued

Pitch Shape vs LHH

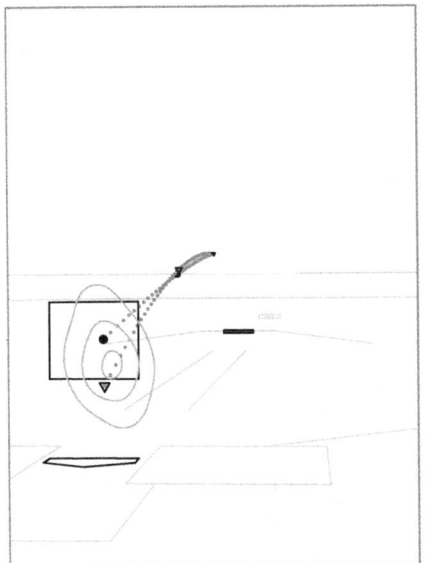

Pitch Shape vs RHH

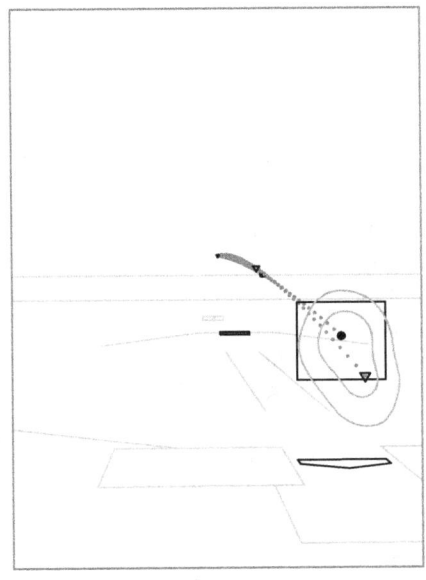

Type	Frequency	Velocity	H Movement	V Movement
● Fastball	39.7%	92.3 [100]	-2.6 [119]	-13.5 [106]
☐ Sinker				
+ Cutter				
▲ Changeup				
✕ Splitter				
▽ Slider	60.3%	82.7 [93]	6 [104]	-34.5 [96]
◇ Curveball				
⊕ Slow Curveball				
✹ Knuckleball				
▼ Screwball				

Corey Kluber RHP

Born: 04/10/86   Age: 34   Bats: R   Throws: R
Height: 6'4"   Weight: 215   Origin: Round 4, 2007 Draft (#134 overall)

YEAR	TEAM	LVL	AGE	W	L	SV	G	GS	IP	H	HR	BB/9	K/9	K	GB%	BABIP
2017	CLE	MLB	31	18	4	0	29	29	203^2	141	21	1.6	11.7	265	46%	.267
2018	CLE	MLB	32	20	7	0	33	33	215	179	25	1.4	9.3	222	46%	.276
2019	CLE	MLB	33	2	3	0	7	7	35^2	44	4	3.8	9.6	38	41%	.370
2020	TEX	MLB	34	11	9	0	28	28	168	159	27	2.6	9.7	181	43%	.298

Comparables: Jeremy Hefner, Collin McHugh, Carlos Carrasco

Sustaining dominance ain't easy. That might seem obvious, but the sport is full of former All-Star hurlers who woke up one day and just didn't have It anymore. Our guess is that Kluber will rebound (even the best robots malfunction on occasion), but he's about to turn 34 and is coming off a rotten go. The two-time Cy Young winner saw his 2019 cut short by a fractured forearm and oblique strain, but he wasn't all that good before landing on the injured list; he walked more batters than ever, resulting in a WHIP—hey, stick with us here—that was more befitting of a swingman. After being traded to Texas in exchange for an intriguing relief arm and the ever-elusive financial flexibility, Kluber will look to be rebooted in a new ballpark and a new division. Here's hoping it's a good one, and that in a year we're writing about how easy the decision was to pick up his $18-million option for 2021.

YEAR	TEAM	LVL	AGE	WHIP	ERA	DRA	WARP	MPH	FB%	WHF	CSP
2017	CLE	MLB	31	0.87	2.25	2.28	7.5	94.2	42.4	16.4	47.2
2018	CLE	MLB	32	0.99	2.89	2.84	6.1	93.8	41.6	13	46.4
2019	CLE	MLB	33	1.65	5.80	6.19	-0.2	93.4	39.8	13.4	43.7
2020	TEX	MLB	34	1.24	4.02	4.04	2.8	92.8	41.1	14.1	44.8

Corey Kluber, continued

Pitch Shape vs LHH

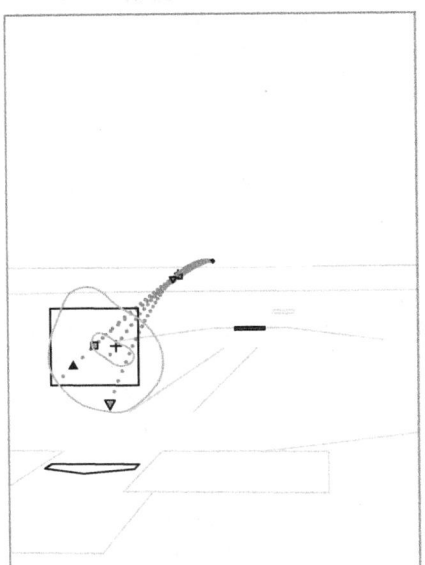

Pitch Shape vs RHH

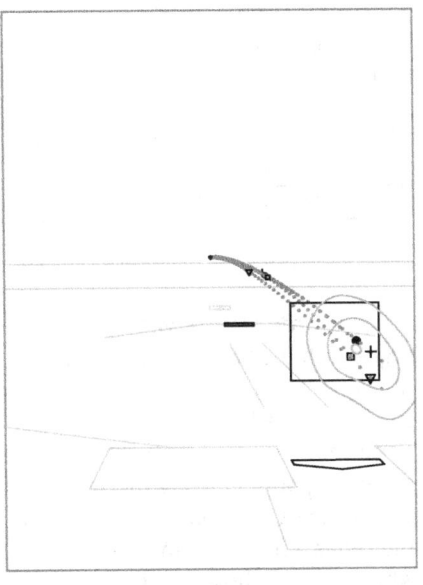

Type	Frequency	Velocity	H Movement	V Movement
● Fastball	13.3%	92.3 [100]	-7.3 [98]	-16.1 [99]
□ Sinker	26.5%	91.9 [96]	-13.6 [94]	-21.7 [95]
+ Cutter	29.0%	88.5 [99]	3.2 [108]	-25.5 [95]
▲ Changeup	8.3%	85.3 [100]	-12.9 [92]	-29.4 [94]
✕ Splitter				
▽ Slider	22.9%	83.3 [95]	15.9 [145]	-35.7 [93]
◇ Curveball				
⊕ Slow Curveball				
✳ Knuckleball				
▼ Screwball				

Derek Law RHP

Born: 09/14/90   Age: 29   Bats: R   Throws: R
Height: 6'3"   Weight: 215   Origin: Round 9, 2011 Draft (#297 overall)

YEAR	TEAM	LVL	AGE	W	L	SV	G	GS	IP	H	HR	BB/9	K/9	K	GB%	BABIP
2017	SAC	AAA	26	1	1	10	25	0	32^2	32	1	3.3	7.2	26	52%	.316
2017	SFN	MLB	26	4	1	4	41	0	37^1	45	5	3.4	8.4	35	40%	.357
2018	SAC	AAA	27	1	3	8	33	0	40^2	34	2	2.0	9.5	43	49%	.305
2018	SFN	MLB	27	1	0	0	7	0	13^1	16	2	5.4	8.1	12	42%	.326
2019	BUF	AAA	28	2	1	2	8	0	10^2	7	1	2.5	14.3	17	50%	.286
2019	TOR	MLB	28	1	2	5	58	4	60^2	61	8	5.9	9.9	67	51%	.317
2020	TOR	MLB	29	2	2	0	33	0	35	32	4	3.9	9.2	36	49%	.291

Comparables: Evan Scribner, Nick Wittgren, Josh Lueke

Law and Order: Derek was never the most obvious spin-off, but it was hard to argue with the San Francisco-set series after seeing its performance in prime time upon its debut in 2016. Since then, ratings have faltered, and in April a surprise move to Toronto was announced in the hopes of enlivening flagging performance. Law (for short) appeared in 58 Toronto games (industry term for episodes), but following the series from San Francisco was inconsistent performance and shaky control. Just because channel Six didn't want to renew the series doesn't mean it's cancelled for good, but the pressure is on to do what so many shows couldn't: break out of old patterns.

YEAR	TEAM	LVL	AGE	WHIP	ERA	DRA	WARP	MPH	FB%	WHF	CSP
2017	SAC	AAA	26	1.35	2.48	3.62	0.6				
2017	SFN	MLB	26	1.58	5.06	4.73	0.2	96.1	54	10.9	46.3
2018	SAC	AAA	27	1.06	4.20	2.91	1.0				
2018	SFN	MLB	27	1.80	7.43	3.72	0.2	96.5	51.6	11.3	44.7
2019	BUF	AAA	28	0.94	1.69	1.63	0.5				
2019	TOR	MLB	28	1.66	4.90	5.48	-0.1	96.5	36.7	12.5	42.7
2020	TOR	MLB	29	1.34	4.04	4.06	0.4	95.7	42.1	12	44.2

Derek Law, continued

Pitch Shape vs LHH

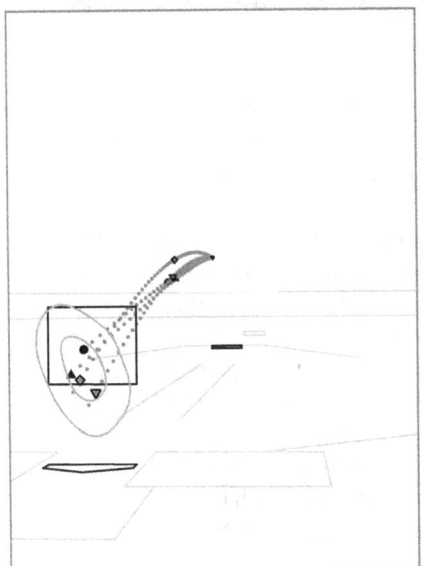

Pitch Shape vs RHH

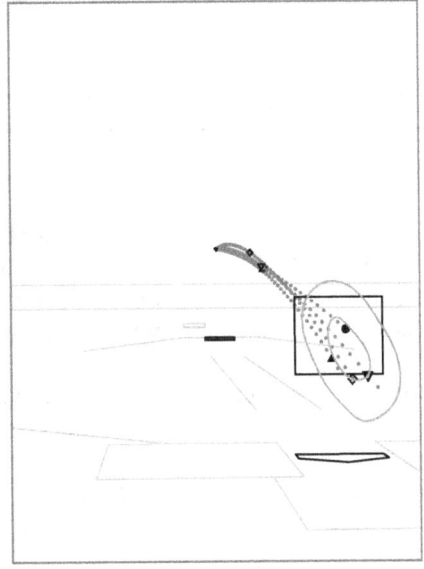

Type	Frequency	Velocity	H Movement	V Movement
● Fastball	36.7%	94.4 [106]	-2.8 [118]	-14.2 [105]
☐ Sinker				
+ Cutter				
▲ Changeup	13.0%	86.2 [103]	-13.1 [91]	-24 [110]
✕ Splitter				
▽ Slider	30.8%	85 [102]	4 [96]	-36.8 [89]
◇ Curveball	19.4%	77 [95]	3.2 [83]	-50.4 [94]
⊕ Slow Curveball				
✳ Knuckleball				
▼ Screwball				

José Leclerc RHP
Born: 12/19/93   Age: 26   Bats: R   Throws: R
Height: 6'0"   Weight: 190   Origin: International Free Agent, 2010

YEAR	TEAM	LVL	AGE	W	L	SV	G	GS	IP	H	HR	BB/9	K/9	K	GB%	BABIP
2017	TEX	MLB	23	2	3	2	47	0	45²	23	4	7.9	11.8	60	40%	.204
2018	TEX	MLB	24	2	3	12	59	0	57²	24	1	3.9	13.3	85	34%	.211
2019	TEX	MLB	25	2	4	14	70	3	68²	52	7	5.1	13.1	100	38%	.306
2020	TEX	MLB	26	3	2	29	52	0	55	41	7	5.8	13.9	84	37%	.305

Comparables: Eduardo Sanchez, Armando Benitez, Matt Mantei

Leclerc was an absolute assassin after taking over the closer's role in 2018. Unfortunately, at least as far as experts have been able to guess, someone dropped Leclerc on the floor sometime in the offseason, knocking his sights slightly askew and morphing him into a rogue, unmanned fire hose to start 2019. After 10 games, Leclerc had a 7.88 ERA, and while he was still striking guys out (nine in eight innings), he also walked seven, including four Astros in two-thirds of an inning on April 26. That was his last night in the closer's role for awhile, as new manager Chris Woodward gave him a few months to get straightened out. He eventually did so, regaining the ninth inning by season's end, which makes him the presumptive favorite to start 2020 there again.

YEAR	TEAM	LVL	AGE	WHIP	ERA	DRA	WARP	MPH	FB%	WHF	CSP
2017	TEX	MLB	23	1.38	3.94	4.65	0.3	97.6	50.9	16.6	39.3
2018	TEX	MLB	24	0.85	1.56	2.87	1.4	97.8	47.8	19	44.2
2019	TEX	MLB	25	1.33	4.33	3.00	1.8	98.8	50.2	14.5	43.4
2020	TEX	MLB	26	1.39	3.99	3.80	0.8	97.9	50.5	16.5	43.4

José Leclerc, continued

Pitch Shape vs LHH

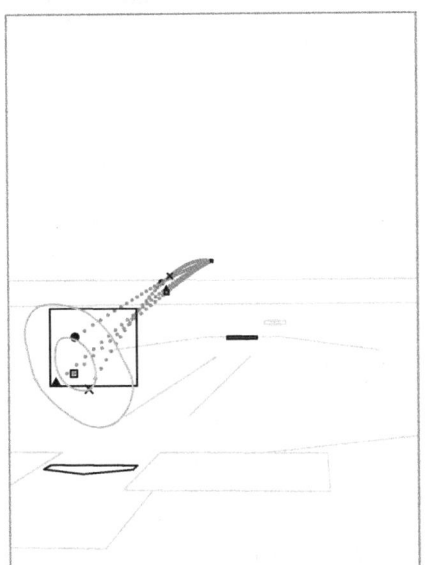

Pitch Shape vs RHH

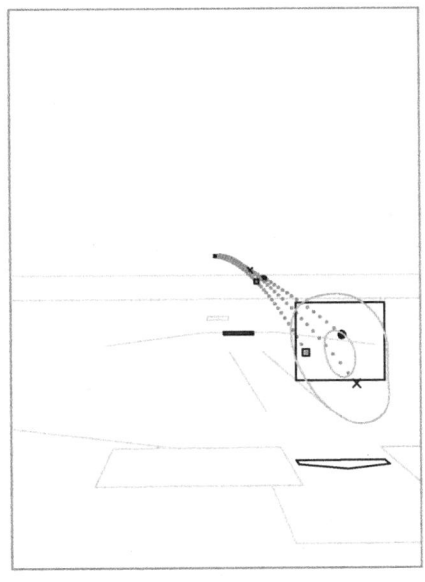

Type	Frequency	Velocity	H Movement	V Movement
● Fastball	41.4%	97 [113]	-2.5 [120]	-11.1 [113]
□ Sinker	8.8%	96.3 [119]	-11.8 [105]	-17.2 [111]
+ Cutter				
▲ Changeup	11.5%	90 [117]	-11.7 [98]	-20.7 [120]
✕ Splitter	35.4%	82.2 [88]	9.5 [165]	-35.8 [78]
▽ Slider				
◇ Curveball				
✧ Slow Curveball				
✱ Knuckleball				
▼ Screwball				

Jordan Lyles RHP

Born: 10/19/90 Age: 29 Bats: R Throws: R
Height: 6'5" Weight: 230 Origin: Round 1, 2008 Draft (#38 overall)

YEAR	TEAM	LVL	AGE	W	L	SV	G	GS	IP	H	HR	BB/9	K/9	K	GB%	BABIP
2017	ELP	AAA	26	1	1	0	5	5	20	20	1	3.6	9.0	20	48%	.333
2017	COL	MLB	26	0	2	0	33	0	46²	61	11	2.3	6.4	33	52%	.331
2017	SDN	MLB	26	1	3	0	5	5	23	35	5	3.9	8.6	22	46%	.395
2018	SDN	MLB	27	2	4	0	24	8	71¹	71	12	2.4	7.8	62	47%	.286
2018	MIL	MLB	27	1	0	0	11	0	16¹	12	0	5.0	12.1	22	42%	.316
2019	MIL	MLB	28	7	1	0	11	11	58²	43	9	3.4	8.6	56	41%	.225
2019	PIT	MLB	28	5	7	0	17	17	82¹	88	16	3.6	9.8	90	43%	.326
2020	TEX	MLB	29	7	7	0	47	16	114	119	19	3.7	9.1	115	42%	.314

Comparables: Jacob Turner, Chris Volstad, Martín Pérez

The seller's remorse kicked in quickly for the Brewers on Lyles, who was let go by Milwaukee after the curveball the club added to his repertoire failed to make a big impact on his results. Turned out all they had to do was wait a bit. Lyles' surface numbers with Pittsburgh were rough, but he flashed a great strikeout rate and was largely the victim of an elevated home-run rate. In acquiring him at the deadline, the Brewers made the correct bet that the home-run bug wouldn't bite him quite so hard in the second half of the season. Lyles will be just 29 in 2020, and the Rangers felt good enough about his chances of sustaining his new level of performance to hand him a two-year pact.

YEAR	TEAM	LVL	AGE	WHIP	ERA	DRA	WARP	MPH	FB%	WHF	CSP
2017	ELP	AAA	26	1.40	4.50	4.08	0.4				
2017	COL	MLB	26	1.56	6.94	5.61	-0.2	96.4	56.7	10.1	48.5
2017	SDN	MLB	26	1.96	9.39	4.14	0.3	94.9	53.3	10.9	43.3
2018	SDN	MLB	27	1.26	4.29	5.91	-0.6	96.3	48.8	10.2	50.2
2018	MIL	MLB	27	1.29	3.31	2.57	0.5	96.7	47.6	14.5	46.6
2019	MIL	MLB	28	1.11	2.45	3.83	1.2	94.3	50.6	10.2	44.8
2019	PIT	MLB	28	1.47	5.36	4.51	1.1	94.7	52.9	11.5	46
2020	TEX	MLB	29	1.45	5.06	4.81	0.8	94.6	51.7	10.9	47.1

Jordan Lyles, continued

Pitch Shape vs LHH

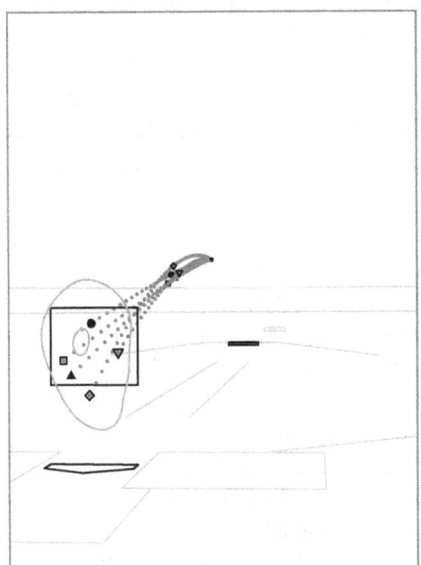

Pitch Shape vs RHH

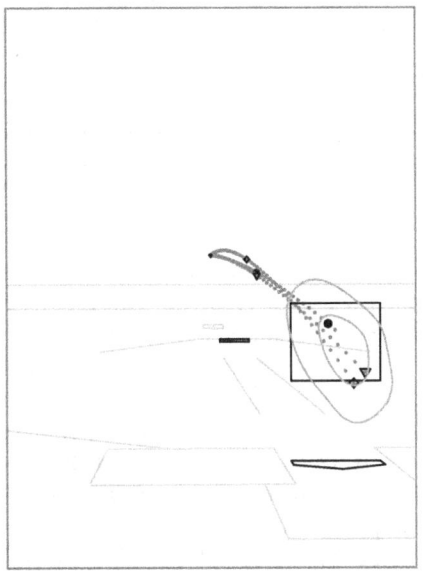

Type	Frequency	Velocity	H Movement	V Movement
● Fastball	50.1%	93 [102]	-5.8 [105]	-13.3 [107]
□ Sinker				
+ Cutter				
▲ Changeup	6.9%	86 [103]	-11.9 [97]	-26.6 [102]
✕ Splitter				
▽ Slider	9.7%	87.8 [115]	4.4 [97]	-26.3 [119]
◇ Curveball	31.3%	81 [108]	5.6 [92]	-50.2 [95]
✥ Slow Curveball				
✳ Knuckleball				
▼ Screwball				

Lance Lynn RHP

Born: 05/12/87 Age: 33 Bats: B Throws: R
Height: 6'5" Weight: 280 Origin: Round 1, 2008 Draft (#39 overall)

YEAR	TEAM	LVL	AGE	W	L	SV	G	GS	IP	H	HR	BB/9	K/9	K	GB%	BABIP
2017	SLN	MLB	30	11	8	0	33	33	186^1	151	27	3.8	7.4	153	45%	.244
2018	MIN	MLB	31	7	8	0	20	20	102^1	105	12	5.5	8.8	100	51%	.322
2018	NYA	MLB	31	3	2	0	11	9	54^1	58	2	2.3	10.1	61	47%	.364
2019	TEX	MLB	32	16	11	0	33	33	208^1	195	21	2.5	10.6	246	41%	.322
2020	TEX	MLB	33	11	9	0	29	29	175	170	23	3.3	10.4	201	42%	.321

Comparables: Tyson Ross, Andrew Cashner, Ian Kennedy

Sometimes reclamation projects go the way of Drew Smyly (2019) or Shelby Miller (2019) or Tyson Ross (2017) or Tim Lincecum (2018) or Edinson Vólquez (2018-19) or Matt Moore (2018) or Kyle Lohse (2016) or Dillon Gee (2017) or Doug Fister (2018). Other times, they end up like Bartolo Colón (2018) or Yovani Gallardo (2018), and if you're lucky, you'll find the occasional Andrew Cashner (2017). But it's extremely rare to sign free agents who provide the sort of surprising value generated by Mike Minor (2018-19) and Lynn (2019). Both pitchers struck out over 200 batters in 2019, the first time Texas has had two 200-plus strikeout guys since Nolan Ryan and Bobby Witt in 1990, though they did it with two completely different styles: Minor is the finesse lefty, while Lynn would throw 200 fastballs per game if the manager allowed it. Fortunately for Lynn and the Rangers, the manager didn't allow it, and after a rough start, Lynn's improved pitch selection vaulted him to what should have been a Cy Young finalist nod.

YEAR	TEAM	LVL	AGE	WHIP	ERA	DRA	WARP	MPH	FB%	WHF	CSP
2017	SLN	MLB	30	1.23	3.43	4.98	1.2	94.4	81	10.1	46
2018	MIN	MLB	31	1.63	5.10	5.53	-0.3	95.8	77	10.8	42.6
2018	NYA	MLB	31	1.33	4.14	4.32	0.6	95.5	77	11.2	46.9
2019	TEX	MLB	32	1.22	3.67	3.15	5.9	96.6	71.5	13.9	49.4
2020	TEX	MLB	33	1.34	4.24	4.11	2.8	94.7	74.6	11.9	46.2

Lance Lynn, continued

Pitch Shape vs LHH

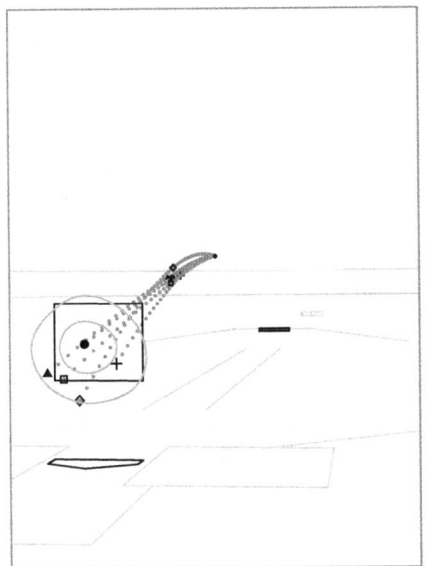

Pitch Shape vs RHH

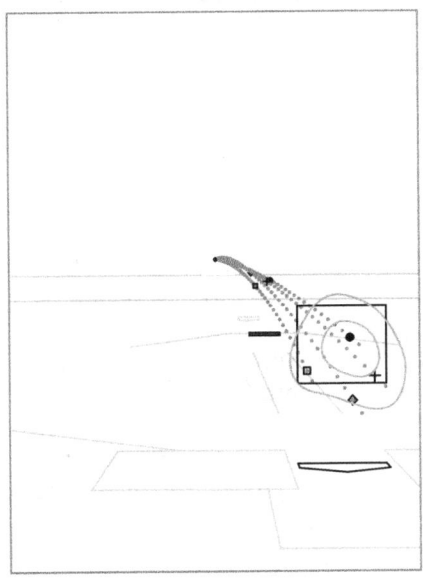

Type	Frequency	Velocity	H Movement	V Movement
● Fastball	54.2%	94.9 [107]	-5.3 [107]	-14.3 [104]
□ Sinker	17.3%	93.1 [103]	-11.3 [109]	-22 [94]
+ Cutter	16.1%	89.3 [104]	3.1 [107]	-26 [93]
▲ Changeup				
✕ Splitter				
▽ Slider				
◇ Curveball	9.6%	81.4 [109]	7.1 [98]	-45.7 [104]
✦ Slow Curveball				
✳ Knuckleball				
▼ Screwball				

Brett Martin LHP

Born: 04/28/95 Age: 25 Bats: L Throws: L
Height: 6'4" Weight: 190 Origin: Round 4, 2014 Draft (#126 overall)

YEAR	TEAM	LVL	AGE	W	L	SV	G	GS	IP	H	HR	BB/9	K/9	K	GB%	BABIP
2017	DEB	A+	22	4	8	0	16	16	84^1	94	7	3.7	9.6	90	47%	.366
2018	FRI	AA	23	2	10	0	29	15	89	138	7	2.9	9.7	96	50%	.443
2019	NAS	AAA	24	0	0	1	10	0	12^2	10	0	2.8	13.5	19	57%	.357
2019	TEX	MLB	24	2	3	0	51	2	62^1	72	7	2.6	9.0	62	53%	.340
2020	TEX	MLB	25	2	2	0	41	0	44	44	5	3.0	8.9	43	51%	.316

Comparables: Jesus Tinoco, Elieser Hernandez, Keury Mella

One interesting thing about Martin's 2019 season was his home/away splits. While Globe Life Park was generally considered a hitter's park, Martin held opponents to a .676 OPS in Arlington. On the road, it was another story altogether, with opponents racking up a mark of .860 (Ironically, Martin had a win-loss record of 0-3 at home and 2-0 on the road. Yay, pitcher wins!). Jumble it together, and Martin was a microcosm of the 2019 Rangers: a few light-bulb moments of inspired progress sprinkled throughout the long, dark summer of learning (or "process", in the parlance of the day). Texas has a fairly left-handed herd of young starting pitchers (Kolby Allard, Taylor Hearn, Joe Palumbo, Brock Burke) but their up-and-coming relief corps are mostly starboard-side, so Martin will get every opportunity to succeed with the organization.

YEAR	TEAM	LVL	AGE	WHIP	ERA	DRA	WARP	MPH	FB%	WHF	CSP
2017	DEB	A+	22	1.53	4.70	6.53	-1.3				
2018	FRI	AA	23	1.88	7.28	7.08	-1.9				
2019	NAS	AAA	24	1.11	0.71	1.84	0.5				
2019	TEX	MLB	24	1.44	4.76	4.45	0.6	95.8	52.2	14.2	49.4
2020	TEX	MLB	25	1.34	4.19	4.10	0.5	95.5	53.4	14.5	50.6

Brett Martin, continued

Pitch Shape vs LHH

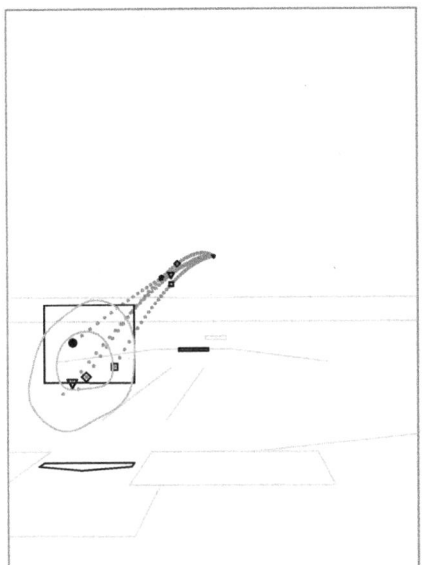

Pitch Shape vs RHH

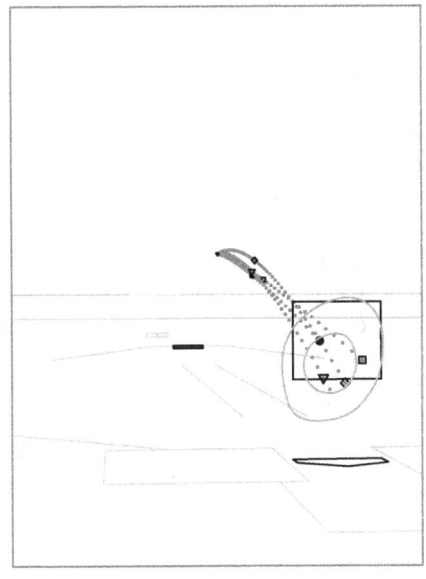

Type	Frequency	Velocity	H Movement	V Movement
● Fastball	30.1%	94.3 [105]	2.4 [120]	-14.4 [104]
☐ Sinker	22.0%	93.9 [107]	10.4 [115]	-19 [105]
+ Cutter				
▲ Changeup				
✕ Splitter				
▽ Slider	33.3%	85.4 [104]	-2.5 [90]	-33.2 [100]
◇ Curveball	14.5%	81.2 [108]	-2.3 [79]	-45.8 [104]
⊕ Slow Curveball				
✳ Knuckleball				
▼ Screwball				

Rangers Player Analysis - 83

Mike Minor LHP

Born: 12/26/87 Age: 32 Bats: R Throws: L
Height: 6'4" Weight: 210 Origin: Round 1, 2009 Draft (#7 overall)

YEAR	TEAM	LVL	AGE	W	L	SV	G	GS	IP	H	HR	BB/9	K/9	K	GB%	BABIP
2017	KCA	MLB	29	6	6	6	65	0	77²	57	5	2.5	10.2	88	43%	.272
2018	TEX	MLB	30	12	8	0	28	28	157	138	25	2.2	7.6	132	35%	.259
2019	TEX	MLB	31	14	10	0	32	32	208¹	190	30	2.9	8.6	200	42%	.287
2020	TEX	MLB	32	11	10	0	29	29	175	172	30	2.9	8.6	167	40%	.293

Comparables: Jaime García, Alex Cobb, Denny Neagle

It's hard to mention Minor without Lance Lynn (or vice versa), since the tandem became the first two Rangers starters to strike out 200+ hitters in the same season since Nolan Ryan and Bobby Witt in 1990. Of course, Minor's 200th strikeout came after Ronald Guzmán intentionally let a foul ball drop in Minor's last inning, prompting the entire baseball world to lose their dang minds for awhile. "Ask me if I care, Pete" became a whole thing for a day (which is now the lifespan of these kinds of stories) and t-shirts were made. But it shouldn't be ignored that Minor's comeback is now firmly established. A year in the bullpen in Kansas City, a year with the reins pulled tight in Texas, and now a full season of dominance. Like Lynn, his pitch selection played a big part of his success in 2019—he became less predictable and relied on an inside-corner changeup that baffled right-handed hitters all season long. Why the Yankees didn't trade for him remains perhaps the greatest mystery of 2019.

YEAR	TEAM	LVL	AGE	WHIP	ERA	DRA	WARP	MPH	FB%	WHF	CSP
2017	KCA	MLB	29	1.02	2.55	2.96	1.9	96.5	45.7	13.5	46.5
2018	TEX	MLB	30	1.12	4.18	5.78	-0.9	95.2	49.5	10.9	50.5
2019	TEX	MLB	31	1.24	3.59	4.04	3.9	94.6	44.7	12.6	50
2020	TEX	MLB	32	1.30	4.36	4.31	2.5	94.1	46	12	48.9

Mike Minor, continued

Pitch Shape vs LHH

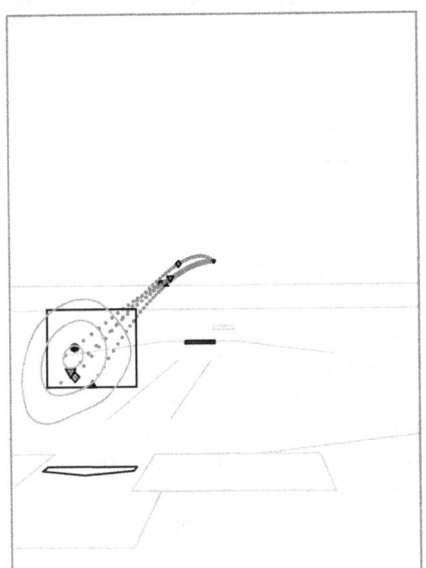

Pitch Shape vs RHH

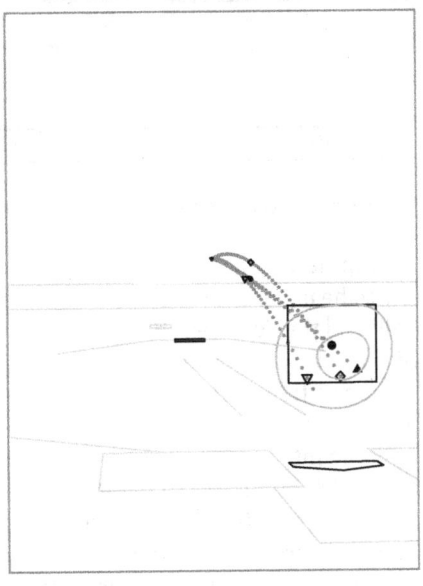

Type	Frequency	Velocity	H Movement	V Movement
● Fastball	44.7%	92.8 [101]	3.7 [114]	-15 [102]
□ Sinker				
+ Cutter				
▲ Changeup	24.6%	86.4 [104]	15.4 [80]	-23 [113]
✕ Splitter				
▽ Slider	19.3%	86.6 [109]	-4.8 [99]	-29.9 [109]
◇ Curveball	11.4%	80.9 [107]	-5.7 [93]	-46.7 [102]
⊕ Slow Curveball				
✻ Knuckleball				
▼ Screwball				

Rafael Montero RHP

Born: 10/17/90 Age: 29 Bats: R Throws: R
Height: 6'0" Weight: 185 Origin: International Free Agent, 2011

YEAR	TEAM	LVL	AGE	W	L	SV	G	GS	IP	H	HR	BB/9	K/9	K	GB%	BABIP
2017	LVG	AAA	26	0	2	0	5	5	29	18	3	3.7	11.5	37	52%	.238
2017	NYN	MLB	26	5	11	0	34	18	119	141	12	5.1	8.6	114	50%	.366
2019	FRI	AA	28	0	0	0	5	2	9	15	0	2.0	15.0	15	26%	.556
2019	TEX	MLB	28	2	0	0	22	0	29	23	5	1.6	10.6	34	40%	.269
2020	TEX	MLB	29	2	2	5	41	0	44	42	6	4.1	10.3	50	42%	.314

Comparables: Kevin Gausman, Jake Faria, A.J. Cole

Fans in New York might remember Montero as the Hank Majewski of the Mets (since he never could quite cut it in the four seasons there (yes, this is a Frankie Valli and the Four Seasons reference, you can "okay boomer" us any time now)). After Tommy John surgery sidelined him for the entire 2018 season, Montero became a free agent, quietly signing a minor-league deal with the Rangers in January of 2019 to absolutely zero fanfare. By July 3, having completed a rehab assignment, he was in Double-A Frisco. By July 19, he was a member of the Nashville Sounds, and a mere three days later, he was called up to the big leagues, where he had his most successful season to date. By that time, the Rangers were out of contention, so there wasn't much buzz about his triumphant return to the majors, but the numbers were real, and so was his fastball.

YEAR	TEAM	LVL	AGE	WHIP	ERA	DRA	WARP	MPH	FB%	WHF	CSP
2017	LVG	AAA	26	1.03	2.48	1.87	1.2				
2017	NYN	MLB	26	1.75	5.52	4.67	1.1	95.7	55.5	10.9	44.2
2019	FRI	AA	28	1.89	7.00	6.24	-0.2				
2019	TEX	MLB	28	0.97	2.48	4.22	0.4	97.5	46.8	13.9	45.2
2020	TEX	MLB	29	1.41	4.43	4.23	0.5	95.5	53.3	11.7	44.8

Rafael Montero, continued

Pitch Shape vs LHH

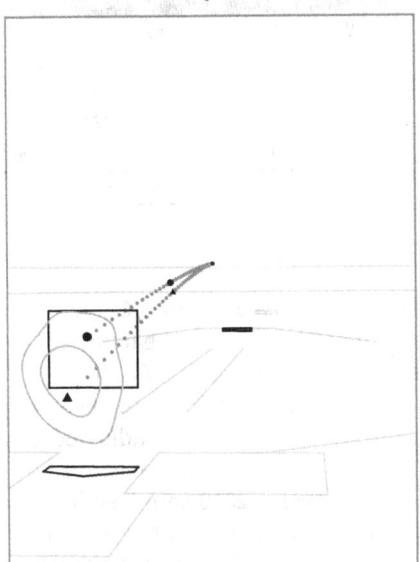

Pitch Shape vs RHH

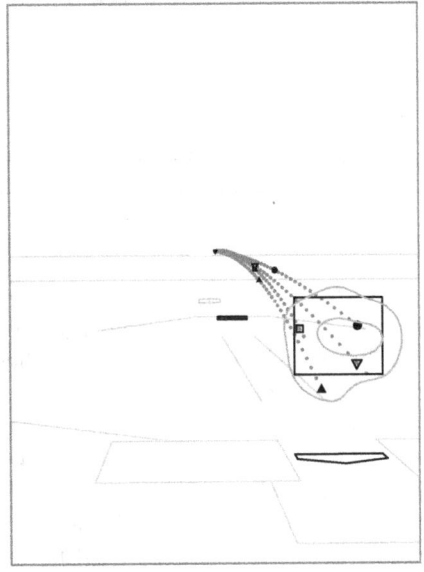

Type	Frequency	Velocity	H Movement	V Movement
● Fastball	39.0%	96 [110]	-8.7 [92]	-14 [105]
□ Sinker	7.8%	95.4 [114]	-12.9 [98]	-18.7 [106]
+ Cutter				
▲ Changeup	39.4%	90 [117]	-14.2 [86]	-25.6 [105]
✕ Splitter				
▽ Slider	13.7%	85.1 [103]	7.2 [109]	-32.6 [101]
◇ Curveball				
✦ Slow Curveball				
✳ Knuckleball				
▼ Screwball				

Texas Rangers 2020

Juan Nicasio RHP
Born: 08/31/86 Age: 33 Bats: R Throws: R
Height: 6'4" Weight: 252 Origin: International Free Agent, 2006

YEAR	TEAM	LVL	AGE	W	L	SV	G	GS	IP	H	HR	BB/9	K/9	K	GB%	BABIP
2017	PIT	MLB	30	2	5	2	65	0	60	49	4	2.7	9.0	60	47%	.285
2017	PHI	MLB	30	1	0	0	2	0	1¹	0	0	0.0	6.8	1	100%	.000
2017	SLN	MLB	30	2	0	4	9	0	11	9	1	1.6	9.0	11	39%	.267
2018	SEA	MLB	31	1	6	1	46	0	42	53	6	1.1	11.4	53	37%	.402
2019	PHI	MLB	32	2	3	1	47	0	47¹	57	4	4.0	8.6	45	48%	.366
2020	PHI	MLB	33	2	2	0	33	0	35	36	6	3.1	8.8	34	44%	.307

Comparables: Carlos Villanueva, Zach McAllister, Bud Norris

Flipped to the Phillies from the Mariners as part of the Jean Segura/Carlos Santana swap, Nicasio had his worst season since 2015, the first year he switched to relieving full time. His believers pointed to his radical ERA/DRA differential in 2018 as a positive sign, but in retrospect a drop in fastball velocity was a harbinger of the ineffectiveness to come. Nicasio eventually adjusted by leaning heavily on his slider and for a brief stretch was somewhat effective but then the Injury Fairy that visited every Phillies reliever in 2019 sprinkled its magic dust on Nicasio in the form of rotator cuff tightness that cut his season short. No matter what happens from this point on for the 32-year-old, the greatest trick he'll ever pull isn't getting someone to chase his slider but earning nearly $30 million while being a replacement-level pitcher for his career.

YEAR	TEAM	LVL	AGE	WHIP	ERA	DRA	WARP	MPH	FB%	WHF	CSP
2017	PIT	MLB	30	1.12	2.85	3.63	1.0	97.7	72.8	12	51.5
2017	PHI	MLB	30	0.00	0.00	5.22	0.0	98.3	45	20	59.7
2017	SLN	MLB	30	1.00	1.64	4.12	0.1	97.8	71.7	13.4	50.3
2018	SEA	MLB	31	1.38	6.00	2.73	1.1	96.6	70.7	12.2	51
2019	PHI	MLB	32	1.65	4.75	5.36	0.0	96.3	54.5	10.2	48.5
2020	PHI	MLB	33	1.36	4.61	4.68	0.3	95.8	64.2	11.3	49.5

Juan Nicasio, continued

Pitch Shape vs LHH

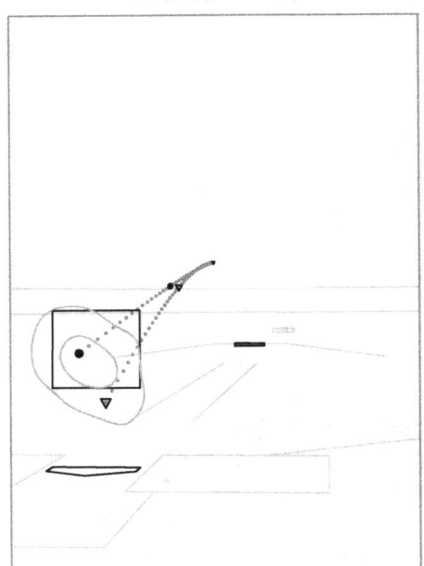

Pitch Shape vs RHH

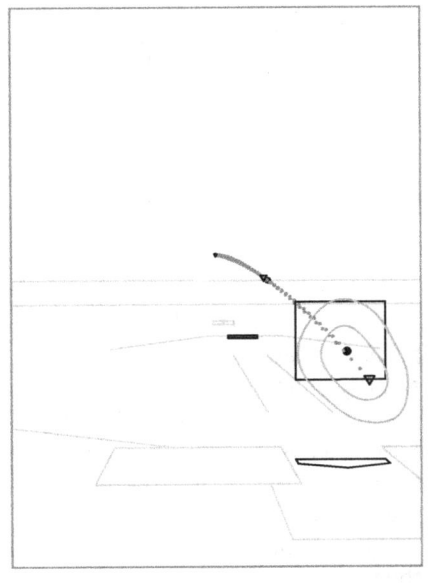

Type	Frequency	Velocity	H Movement	V Movement
● Fastball	50.3%	94.1 [105]	-8.4 [93]	-14.4 [104]
□ Sinker	4.2%	92.7 [100]	-13.1 [97]	-18 [109]
+ Cutter				
▲ Changeup				
✕ Splitter				
▽ Slider	44.9%	87 [111]	2.2 [88]	-27.6 [116]
◇ Curveball				
✦ Slow Curveball				
✳ Knuckleball				
▼ Screwball				

Joe Palumbo LHP

Born: 10/26/94 Age: 25 Bats: L Throws: L
Height: 6'1" Weight: 168 Origin: Round 30, 2013 Draft (#910 overall)

YEAR	TEAM	LVL	AGE	W	L	SV	G	GS	IP	H	HR	BB/9	K/9	K	GB%	BABIP
2017	DEB	A+	22	1	0	0	3	3	13^2	4	0	2.6	14.5	22	58%	.167
2018	DEB	A+	23	1	4	0	6	6	27	24	3	2.0	11.3	34	42%	.304
2018	FRI	AA	23	1	0	0	2	2	9^1	6	0	2.9	9.6	10	39%	.261
2019	FRI	AA	24	0	0	0	11	10	53^2	43	5	4.2	11.6	69	41%	.309
2019	NAS	AAA	24	3	0	0	6	6	27	13	4	3.3	13.0	39	40%	.188
2019	TEX	MLB	24	0	3	0	7	4	16^2	21	7	4.3	11.3	21	36%	.326
2020	TEX	MLB	25	2	3	0	34	3	45	47	9	3.4	7.9	39	38%	.294

Comparables: Thomas Pannone, Antonio Bastardo, Jarlin García

There's this weird sandwich happening with Palumbo's baseball career. One piece of bread is the kid who was drafted in the 30th round after an eligibility snafu left him pitching in a semi-pro men's league as a high school senior. Not exactly the recipe for an All-Star, right? A feel-good story, sure. An underdog? Absolutely. A can't-miss prospect? Ehhhh…The other piece of bread is Palumbo's 2019 season. Blisters and bats made it quite a lesson in—what was it that Calvin's dad used to call it in the comic strip—character building? Look at that line. That's a 30th-round draft pick's line if ever you've seen one. And yet, the meat of the sandwich is that Palumbo has become a for-real prospect who was laying waste to High-A batters in 2017 before the dreaded Tommy John surgery came to call, then worked his way back to enough success in 2018 that his major-league debut in 2019 was something of a foregone conclusion. Yeah, 2019 was an exercise in things going pear-shaped, but Palumbo has enough juice to make himself a starter of interest when pitchers and catchers report (and beyond).

YEAR	TEAM	LVL	AGE	WHIP	ERA	DRA	WARP	MPH	FB%	WHF	CSP
2017	DEB	A+	22	0.59	0.66	1.48	0.6				
2018	DEB	A+	23	1.11	2.67	4.07	0.4				
2018	FRI	AA	23	0.96	1.93	3.31	0.2				
2019	FRI	AA	24	1.27	3.19	3.60	0.9				
2019	NAS	AAA	24	0.85	2.67	1.78	1.3				
2019	TEX	MLB	24	1.74	9.18	5.67	0.0	95.7	56.7	10	49.8
2020	TEX	MLB	25	1.42	5.30	5.11	0.1	95.4	58	10.2	51

Joe Palumbo, continued

Pitch Shape vs LHH

Pitch Shape vs RHH

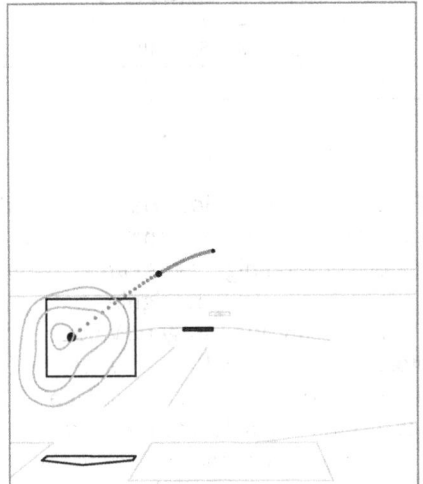
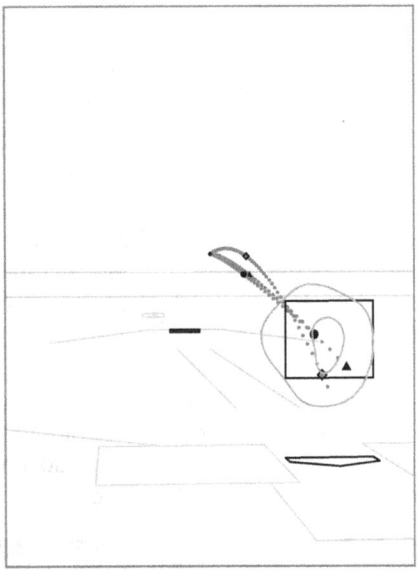

Type	Frequency	Velocity	H Movement	V Movement
● Fastball	56.7%	94.2 [105]	5.7 [105]	-13.1 [107]
☐ Sinker				
+ Cutter				
▲ Changeup	17.6%	87.3 [107]	7.7 [116]	-24.7 [108]
✕ Splitter				
▽ Slider				
◇ Curveball	24.5%	79 [101]	-8.8 [105]	-49.6 [96]
✦ Slow Curveball				
✸ Knuckleball				
▼ Screwball				

Edinson Vólquez   RHP
Born: 07/03/83   Age: 36   Bats: R   Throws: R
Height: 6'0"   Weight: 220   Origin: International Free Agent, 2001

YEAR	TEAM	LVL	AGE	W	L	SV	G	GS	IP	H	HR	BB/9	K/9	K	GB%	BABIP
2017	MIA	MLB	33	4	8	0	17	17	92¹	78	8	5.2	7.9	81	49%	.278
2019	TEX	MLB	35	0	1	0	11	4	16	20	3	6.8	5.6	10	45%	.340
2020	TEX	MLB	36	2	2	0	33	0	35	37	5	4.4	7.8	30	47%	.311

Comparables: Ubaldo Jiménez, Bobby Witt, Edwin Jackson

The Rangers once traded Vólquez to the Cincinnati Reds for Josh Hamilton. That worked out great for them, but—while Vólquez wasn't quite as impactful as Hamilton's best years in Texas—he forged a pretty good big-league career in his own right. He eventually made it full-circle back to the Rangers, signing before the 2018 season while he was recovering from Tommy John surgery. Vólquez barely cleared the starting line in 2019 before going down with another elbow injury, and it would have been perfectly understandable if he had called it a career. Instead, the team asked him to stick around and help mentor some of their young pitchers. Vólquez did so, and eventually even made it back to the mound for the end of the season.

YEAR	TEAM	LVL	AGE	WHIP	ERA	DRA	WARP	MPH	FB%	WHF	CSP
2017	MIA	MLB	33	1.42	4.19	4.89	0.7	95.4	56.8	9.5	43.6
2019	TEX	MLB	35	2.00	6.75	6.50	-0.2	96.5	47.8	8.1	46.3
2020	TEX	MLB	36	1.56	5.41	5.19	0.0	94.3	53.4	9	44.3

Edinson Vólquez, continued

Pitch Shape vs LHH

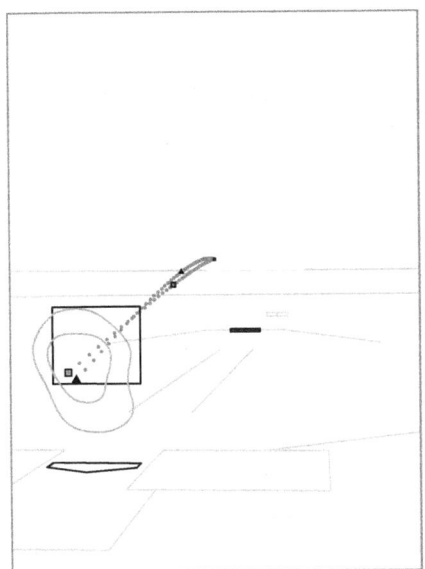

Pitch Shape vs RHH

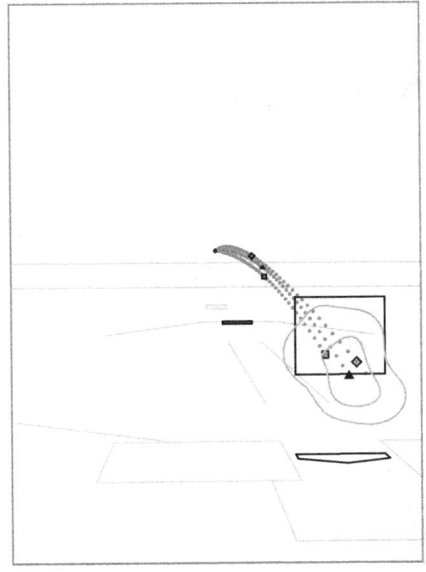

Type	Frequency	Velocity	H Movement	V Movement
● Fastball	14.1%	93.7 [104]	-10.4 [84]	-16.3 [99]
☐ Sinker	33.7%	93.8 [106]	-14.3 [89]	-19 [105]
+ Cutter				
▲ Changeup	36.7%	83.4 [93]	-11.1 [100]	-33.9 [81]
✕ Splitter				
▽ Slider				
◇ Curveball	15.5%	81.1 [108]	8.2 [103]	-45.2 [105]
⊕ Slow Curveball				
✳ Knuckleball				
▼ Screwball				

Rangers Player Analysis - 93

PLAYER COMMENTS WITHOUT GRAPHS

Sherten Apostel 3B
Born: 03/11/99 Age: 21 Bats: R Throws: R
Height: 6'4" Weight: 200 Origin: International Free Agent, 2018

YEAR	TEAM	LVL	AGE	PA	R	2B	3B	HR	RBI	BB	K	SB	CS	AVG/OBP/SLG
2017	DPI	RK	18	259	43	12	4	9	48	56	49	4	5	.258/.422/.495
2018	BRI	RK	19	175	28	7	0	7	26	32	42	3	1	.259/.406/.460
2018	SPO	A-	19	49	7	1	0	1	10	9	8	0	1	.351/.469/.459
2019	HIC	A	20	319	38	13	1	15	43	28	71	2	1	.258/.332/.470
2019	DEB	A+	20	159	18	5	1	4	16	23	49	0	0	.237/.352/.378
2020	TEX	MLB	21	251	27	11	1	8	30	26	82	0	0	.228/.314/.397

Comparables: Yairo Muñoz, Brett Phillips, Drew Robinson

Jamey Newberg of The Athletic brought up an interesting theory about Apostel's 2019 season, which started extremely slowly: "...the Curacao native had never played a pro game earlier than June, and some believe he was so unaccustomed to cool weather that it chilled his production." His output at Hickory definitely seemed to follow that pattern, switching gears mid-May and prompting a promotion to Down East. While the Josh Jung/Davis Wendzel question might be the easier minor league third base conundrum to identify from the outside (both Big 12 co-Players of the year were drafted by the Rangers in 2019), Apostel—who came from Pittsburgh as the PTBNL in the Keone Kela trade—is going to force the issue in 2020. In fact, with Wendzel missing time with a thumb injury, it's Apostel who will force the Rangers to make an interesting decision about which third baseman will start for the Wood Ducks and who will be elsewhere. For Apostel, that might mean Frisco—he was added to the 40-man roster over the offseason, and finished strong in Down East in 2019—or it might be first base.

YEAR	TEAM	LVL	AGE	PA	DRC+	VORP	BABIP	BRR	FRAA	WARP
2017	DPI	RK	18	259	158	37.7	.296	-0.6	3B(59): 8.9	2.9
2018	BRI	RK	19	175	148	12.7	.319	-0.9	3B(35): 3.6	1.7
2018	SPO	A-	19	49	203	9.0	.400	0.0	3B(8): -0.6	0.5
2019	HIC	A	20	319	119	13.7	.290	-3.0	3B(70): 1.6, 1B(12): 0.0	1.4
2019	DEB	A+	20	159	117	9.9	.341	1.6	3B(40): 1.4	1.1
2020	TEX	MLB	21	251	87	3.4	.320	-0.4	3B 2, 1B 0	0.6

Greg Bird 1B

Born: 11/09/92   Age: 27   Bats: L   Throws: R
Height: 6'4"   Weight: 220   Origin: Round 5, 2011 Draft (#179 overall)

YEAR	TEAM	LVL	AGE	PA	R	2B	3B	HR	RBI	BB	K	SB	CS	AVG/OBP/SLG
2017	SWB	AAA	24	59	12	4	0	3	7	11	9	0	0	.298/.424/.574
2017	NYA	MLB	24	170	20	7	0	9	28	19	42	0	0	.190/.288/.422
2018	NYA	MLB	25	311	23	16	1	11	38	30	78	0	0	.199/.286/.386
2019	NYA	MLB	26	41	6	0	0	1	1	6	16	0	0	.171/.293/.257
2020	NYA	MLB	27	251	31	10	0	13	36	29	74	0	0	.222/.318/.443

Comparables: Brandon Nimmo, Daniel Vogelbach, Ryan O'Hearn

An exciting spring training competition with Luke Voit promised great things for Bird's 2019 season. He was back to his true form; with a vengeance; with something to prove. In a lineup that lacked enough of a left-handed presence, Bird's beautiful swing could have been a serious game changer, and he came out of the cage showcasing just that. Unfortunately, Bird has a long resume of could have beens. After a strong burst out of the gate in his rookie season, a shoulder injury cost him all of 2016. Then it was his ankle that sidelined him for most of 2017. A healthy (at least for him) Bird struggled in 2018 and left the door open for Voit to make his way into the Yankees' long-term plans. This time around he tore his left plantar fascia, limiting him to just a handful of at-bats in his age-26 season. The broken tissue acted as final straw for the organization, as they designated him for assignment in November. Bird remains, as always, with everything left to prove once again.

YEAR	TEAM	LVL	AGE	PA	DRC+	VORP	BABIP	BRR	FRAA	WARP
2017	SWB	AAA	24	59	161	4.5	.306	-1.0	1B(10): 0.9	0.4
2017	NYA	MLB	24	170	99	0.6	.194	-1.0	1B(46): -1.1	0.0
2018	NYA	MLB	25	311	84	-7.9	.230	-1.8	1B(74): 1.4	-0.2
2019	NYA	MLB	26	41	73	-0.9	.278	0.5	1B(10): 0.5	0.0
2020	NYA	MLB	27	251	100	7.6	.271	-0.7	1B 0	0.7

Sam Huff C

Born: 01/14/98 Age: 22 Bats: R Throws: R
Height: 6'4" Weight: 230 Origin: Round 7, 2016 Draft (#219 overall)

YEAR	TEAM	LVL	AGE	PA	R	2B	3B	HR	RBI	BB	K	SB	CS	AVG/OBP/SLG
2017	RNG	RK	19	225	34	9	2	9	31	24	66	3	2	.249/.329/.452
2018	HIC	A	20	448	53	22	3	18	55	23	140	9	1	.241/.292/.439
2019	HIC	A	21	114	22	5	0	15	29	6	37	4	1	.333/.368/.796
2019	DEB	A+	21	405	49	17	2	13	43	27	117	2	5	.262/.326/.425
2020	TEX	MLB	22	251	24	12	1	7	27	16	92	1	0	.219/.277/.364

Comparables: Eric Haase, Isan Díaz, Chris Carter

The question about Huff since forever has been if he'll be able to stick at catcher, since he's 6-foot-4 and getting down into the catcher's squat 150 times a game is like cramming a week's worth of clothes into a backpack and then zipping and unzipping it 150 times over the course of three hours. Huff has thus far proven to be stitched out of iron, wielding an arm made of gunpowder (48 percent caught-stealing rate) and a bat made of kerosene. His strikeout rate is still high enough to temper any legitimate push for the big leagues just yet, but he's still just 21. By catcher standards, that means he's only about 16 years old (and about nine feet tall). He'll likely see a lot of time in Double-A Frisco in 2020, hoping to arrive in Arlington right about the time the Rangers expect to be competitive again.

YEAR	TEAM	LVL	AGE	PA	DRC+	VORP	BABIP	BRR	FRAA	WARP
2017	RNG	RK	19	225	97	14.6	.320	0.7	C(30): -0.5	0.7
2018	HIC	A	20	448	97	14.0	.317	-0.1	C(56): 1.9, 1B(11): -0.4	1.3
2019	HIC	A	21	114	217	22.7	.375	0.8	C(14): 0.9	1.8
2019	DEB	A+	21	405	110	18.4	.347	-2.7	C(50): 1.9, 1B(4): 0.1	1.5
2020	TEX	MLB	22	251	68	-2.6	.328	-0.3	C 1, 1B 0	-0.2

Josh Jung 3B

Born: 02/12/98 Age: 22 Bats: R Throws: R
Height: 6'2" Weight: 215 Origin: Round 1, 2019 Draft (#8 overall)

YEAR	TEAM	LVL	AGE	PA	R	2B	3B	HR	RBI	BB	K	SB	CS	AVG/OBP/SLG
2019	HIC	A	21	179	18	13	0	1	23	16	29	4	1	.287/.363/.389
2020	TEX	MLB	22	251	22	12	1	4	23	15	60	3	1	.233/.288/.343

Comparables: Zelous Wheeler, Ty Kelly, Paul DeJong

You can certainly make an argument that the draft was the weakest of the five means of player acquisition (draft, trade, free agent, Latin American signings, waiver claims) for the Rangers in the early-to-mid 2010s. Sure, it's possible that player development could have been responsible for the busts of Dillon Tate, Chi Chi González, Travis Demeritte, Kevin Matthews, Kellin Deglan, and Jake Skole (all of whom were first-round picks for the Rangers this decade), but the last couple of years have (hopefully) turned the tide a bit. Bubba Thompson, Hans Crouse, Cole Ragans and others have populated the farm system with a hopeful crop of homegrowns.

Jung is the latest cause for optimism. Drafted out of Texas Tech, Jung shared Big 12 co-Player of the Year honors with Baylor's Davis Wendzel, also drafted by Texas in a nifty bit of synergy. He played just four games in the AZL before skipping straight to Low-A. At the end of his first month in Hickory, Jung was hitting over .300 with an on-base percentage of .358, prompting some to wonder if he would find himself in High-A by season's end. He cooled a bit, and his power is still in need of development, but he's still, ahem, Jung.

YEAR	TEAM	LVL	AGE	PA	DRC+	VORP	BABIP	BRR	FRAA	WARP
2019	HIC	A	21	179	137	13.7	.341	0.6	3B(35): 2.5	1.5
2020	TEX	MLB	22	251	70	-1.9	.297	0.0	3B 4	0.3

Chris Seise SS

Born: 01/06/99   Age: 21   Bats: R   Throws: R
Height: 6'2"   Weight: 175   Origin: Round 1, 2017 Draft (#29 overall)

YEAR	TEAM	LVL	AGE	PA	R	2B	3B	HR	RBI	BB	K	SB	CS	AVG/OBP/SLG
2017	RNG	RK	18	129	23	5	3	3	27	9	30	5	0	.336/.395/.509
2017	SPO	A-	18	104	10	3	1	0	9	4	30	1	1	.222/.250/.273
2019	HIC	A	20	92	12	4	3	0	6	3	33	6	5	.241/.272/.356
2020	TEX	MLB	21	251	20	11	2	4	22	13	96	3	1	.213/.260/.319

Comparables: Michael Chavis, Steven Moya, Deivy Grullon

If you're a Rangers prospect nerd who also plays guitar, this comment is for you: Have you had a Line 6 stomp box that was built after 2006? Sorry, let's re-phrase that: How many times have you had to replace your Line 6 stomp box that was built after 2006, after stupidly selling your old one that was still working? For the rest of you: the older pedals were made by a different manufacturer. The new ones broke about once a year if you were playing them regularly. Which was a shame: The Line 6 DL-4 was a fantastic delay/loop pedal! Anyway, if Chris Seise can stay healthy, he's probably going to be a fantastic shortstop. But he's going to need to stay healthy sometime in the near future or the Rangers might have to settle for one with a bit less functionality and a bit more durability.

YEAR	TEAM	LVL	AGE	PA	DRC+	VORP	BABIP	BRR	FRAA	WARP
2017	RNG	RK	18	129	118	14.2	.429	1.4	SS(24): -3.6	0.5
2017	SPO	A-	18	104	51	-1.4	.314	0.5	SS(23): -0.2	0.0
2019	HIC	A	20	92	73	2.5	.382	-0.8	SS(18): -0.3	0.0
2020	TEX	MLB	21	251	55	-6.6	.344	0.1	SS -1	-0.8

Leody Taveras CF

Born: 09/08/98   Age: 21   Bats: B   Throws: R
Height: 6'1"   Weight: 171   Origin: International Free Agent, 2015

YEAR	TEAM	LVL	AGE	PA	R	2B	3B	HR	RBI	BB	K	SB	CS	AVG/OBP/SLG
2017	HIC	A	18	577	73	20	7	8	50	47	92	20	6	.249/.312/.360
2018	DEB	A+	19	580	65	16	7	5	48	51	96	19	11	.246/.312/.332
2019	DEB	A+	20	290	44	7	4	2	25	31	62	21	5	.294/.368/.376
2019	FRI	AA	20	293	32	12	4	3	31	23	60	11	8	.265/.320/.375
2020	TEX	MLB	21	210	18	8	2	3	19	14	53	4	2	.238/.291/.350

Comparables: Engel Beltre, Carlos Tocci, Cheslor Cuthbert

When Taveras had an OPS of .644 in High-A in 2018, the Donald Harris alarm bells started going bonkers in the Rangers' front offices. The "can't miss" prospect was missing, a lot. He still missed a lot in 2019 (122 strikeouts in 519 plate appearances), but he started doing other things well, namely ... hitting. He even held his own against Double-A pitching, so we can check that off the Will This Prospect Be Okay list. Furthermore, he just turned 21 in September, so even if the Texas League proves challenging in 2020, there's time for him to figure things out before the demand for his services in Arlington begins to over-ripen. As for his defense? Well that's never been an issue. He's probably ready to be a big-league center fielder right now, but unless he develops some completely unexpected power surge as he continues to grow into his body, he'll have to cut down on strikeouts before he's ready to face big-league pitching. You have to earn those kind of strikeout numbers by hitting mega-bombs in your other at-bats. Thus far, that does not appear to be the Taveras MO.

YEAR	TEAM	LVL	AGE	PA	DRC+	VORP	BABIP	BRR	FRAA	WARP
2017	HIC	A	18	577	98	16.8	.287	3.3	CF(125): -3.7, LF(3): -0.1	1.6
2018	DEB	A+	19	580	90	4.2	.292	0.3	CF(123): 7.0, RF(3): 0.0	2.0
2019	DEB	A+	20	290	124	14.6	.378	-0.4	CF(34): -0.6, RF(23): 4.0	1.7
2019	FRI	AA	20	293	97	9.2	.327	0.5	CF(64): 8.1	1.8
2020	TEX	MLB	21	210	67	-1.1	.310	0.2	CF 1	0.0

Anderson Tejeda SS

Born: 05/01/98 Age: 22 Bats: B Throws: R
Height: 5'11" Weight: 160 Origin: International Free Agent, 2014

YEAR	TEAM	LVL	AGE	PA	R	2B	3B	HR	RBI	BB	K	SB	CS	AVG/OBP/SLG
2017	HIC	A	19	446	68	24	9	8	53	36	132	10	7	.247/.309/.411
2018	DEB	A+	20	522	76	17	5	19	74	49	142	11	4	.259/.331/.439
2019	DEB	A+	21	181	22	10	1	4	24	17	58	9	4	.234/.315/.386
2020	TEX	MLB	22	251	24	12	2	8	29	15	92	2	1	.219/.270/.393

Comparables: Trevor Story, Yu Chang, Junior Lake

If all you have to go on is the numbers, it would be easy to look at Tejeda's 2019 season as a total bust. Not only did he repeat a level, but his numbers were worse than the previous season, all before a shoulder injury limited him to just 43 games. That's all true, and there's no mitigating the loss of playing time, but perhaps it helps to consider that he started switch-hitting in 2019 (which might have been part of the reason he started the season at High-A Down East). He's got good pop in his bat and is a great defender—enough so that Texas opted to add him to the 40-man roster rather than leave him susceptible to the Rule 5 draft—so assuming he's healthy in 2020, he'll probably get a fair amount of time in Frisco. A lot of the buzz about minor-league competition has been focused on third base, but there's a good chance that the competition for heir apparent to the Elvis Andrus throne will start to get extremely interesting in about two years' time when Tejeda and Chris Seise (not to mention Jonathan Ornelas and Eli White) could be contenders to take over the position in Arlington. Step one: they'll both need to stay healthy.

YEAR	TEAM	LVL	AGE	PA	DRC+	VORP	BABIP	BRR	FRAA	WARP
2017	HIC	A	19	446	93	21.4	.343	2.0	SS(82): -2.0, 2B(30): 0.0	1.4
2018	DEB	A+	20	522	122	29.5	.330	3.0	SS(105): 2.9, 2B(12): 1.6	4.1
2019	DEB	A+	21	181	84	11.5	.333	1.3	SS(39): 2.4	0.8
2020	TEX	MLB	22	251	69	-1.8	.322	0.0	SS 0, 2B 1	-0.1

Bubba Thompson CF

Born: 06/09/98 Age: 22 Bats: R Throws: R
Height: 6'1" Weight: 180 Origin: Round 1, 2017 Draft (#26 overall)

YEAR	TEAM	LVL	AGE	PA	R	2B	3B	HR	RBI	BB	K	SB	CS	AVG/OBP/SLG
2017	RNG	RK	19	123	23	7	2	3	12	6	28	5	5	.257/.317/.434
2018	HIC	A	20	363	52	18	5	8	42	23	104	32	7	.289/.344/.446
2019	DEB	A+	21	228	24	8	2	5	21	21	72	12	3	.178/.261/.312
2020	TEX	MLB	22	251	23	12	1	6	25	14	91	9	3	.205/.259/.344

Comparables: Dexter Fowler, Keon Broxton, Darren Ford

There was a time (and that time was the end of the 2018 season) when some were beginning to wonder if Thompson was going to surpass Leody Taveras in the Rangers center field prospect rankings. Taveras was struggling to find himself at the plate and Thompson was exceeding expectations. Last season proved to be the great evening-out, though Thompson's step back was as much a result of bad luck as anything. First it was a hamate bone, then a foot injury cost him another month. The rest of the season was spent trying to overcome the rustiness that comes with missing a lot of time that would have otherwise been spent developing. Injuries are never "good news" but the ability to attribute Thompson's slow 2019 season to injuries does, in some way, provide a bit of hope that a simple "force-close and re-launch app" will be sufficient in 2020 for the 21-year-old.

YEAR	TEAM	LVL	AGE	PA	DRC+	VORP	BABIP	BRR	FRAA	WARP
2017	RNG	RK	19	123	83	4.0	.317	0.8	CF(27): -4.0	-0.1
2018	HIC	A	20	363	118	26.0	.396	6.1	CF(67): 1.1, LF(17): 0.7	2.6
2019	DEB	A+	21	228	55	-2.9	.246	2.6	LF(33): 1.5, CF(20): -1.8	-0.2
2020	TEX	MLB	22	251	57	-5.0	.307	0.9	CF -1, LF 2	-0.5

Steele Walker OF

Born: 07/30/96 Age: 23 Bats: L Throws: L
Height: 5'11" Weight: 190 Origin: Round 2, 2018 Draft (#46 overall)

YEAR	TEAM	LVL	AGE	PA	R	2B	3B	HR	RBI	BB	K	SB	CS	AVG/OBP/SLG
2018	GRF	RK	21	38	4	1	0	2	4	1	7	1	1	.206/.263/.412
2018	KAN	A	21	126	13	5	0	3	17	8	29	5	1	.186/.246/.310
2019	KAN	A	22	87	6	10	3	0	11	8	15	4	2	.365/.437/.581
2019	WNS	A+	22	441	59	26	2	10	51	42	63	9	5	.269/.346/.426
2020	TEX	MLB	23	251	25	13	1	7	28	14	55	5	2	.228/.280/.385

Comparables: Lane Adams, Kevin Kiermaier, Dave Sappelt

Walker doesn't have top-end speed, so he can appear miscast as a center fielder. A ball stroked to the gap would typically provide a chance to assess an outfielder's ability to close and cover ground. But maybe Walker's hat pops off during his pursuit, his flowing blond locks flutter out like a fan, turned golden by the illumination of the sunlight. The Earth starts to slow, gentle pluckings of a Spanish guitar seem to waft in the air, and is Walker stopping in mid-pursuit to gaze into your eyes? Well…uh…so, the likelihood he ends up in an outfield corner puts more pressure on the bat—while the plate discipline has exceeded some college grades, his stout shorter frame needs to employ a bit more effort in his swing to tap into home-run power. Perhaps the added effort sends his batting helmet flying to the dirt, and revealing his hair again like a thousand glittering blades of dry grass in a meadow, bound together in a sumptuous wave. An appealing vision of a platoon-mashing left fielder comes into conceivable view, and…uh …um…what was the question?

YEAR	TEAM	LVL	AGE	PA	DRC+	VORP	BABIP	BRR	FRAA	WARP
2018	GRF	RK	21	38	74	0.9	.192	0.4	CF(8): -2.0	-0.2
2018	KAN	A	21	126	55	-1.3	.214	0.3	CF(21): 1.2	-0.1
2019	KAN	A	22	87	180	12.9	.443	-0.4	CF(16): -1.7, RF(4): -0.1	0.6
2019	WNS	A+	22	441	126	18.1	.294	-1.0	CF(81): -2.5	2.0
2020	TEX	MLB	23	251	75	-0.1	.268	-0.1	CF -2, RF 0	-0.2

Eli White SS

Born: 06/26/94   Age: 26   Bats: R   Throws: R
Height: 6'2"   Weight: 175   Origin: Round 11, 2016 Draft (#322 overall)

YEAR	TEAM	LVL	AGE	PA	R	2B	3B	HR	RBI	BB	K	SB	CS	AVG/OBP/SLG
2017	STO	A+	23	502	71	32	6	4	36	41	121	12	5	.270/.342/.395
2018	MID	AA	24	578	81	30	8	9	55	62	116	18	9	.306/.388/.450
2019	NAS	AAA	25	499	63	20	5	14	43	43	138	14	5	.253/.337/.418
2020	TEX	MLB	26	140	14	7	1	3	15	10	45	2	1	.242/.310/.388

Comparables: Brian Bixler, Joey Butler, Joey Wendle

When the Rangers traded Jurickson Profar to Oakland in a three-way deal that netted them Brock Burke, Kyle Bird and Yoel Espinal from Tampa, White was a surprisingly valuable get from Oakland. The ability to play multiple positions well—including shortstop and center field—earned him an invitation to big-league camp, and he seemed to have an outside shot at making the club out of spring training. Instead, Logan Forsythe (and later Danny Santana) filled utility roles for Texas while White had a modestly successful season in Triple-A. The Rangers' coming horde of middle infielders made White a bit more expendable when roster-crunch time came in November, and Texas left him vulnerable to the Rule 5 draft.

YEAR	TEAM	LVL	AGE	PA	DRC+	VORP	BABIP	BRR	FRAA	WARP
2017	STO	A+	23	502	104	21.8	.360	-0.2	SS(92): -7.9, CF(8): -1.5	1.2
2018	MID	AA	24	578	134	36.5	.379	3.2	2B(66): 2.8, SS(42): 2.6	4.6
2019	NAS	AAA	25	499	80	17.4	.336	1.7	SS(91): -6.8, CF(22): -0.5	0.6
2020	TEX	MLB	26	140	81	1.5	.346	0.0	CF -1, 2B 0	0.1

Kyle Cody RHP

Born: 08/09/94   Age: 25   Bats: R   Throws: R
Height: 6'7"   Weight: 245   Origin: Round 6, 2016 Draft (#189 overall)

YEAR	TEAM	LVL	AGE	W	L	SV	G	GS	IP	H	HR	BB/9	K/9	K	GB%	BABIP
2017	HIC	A	22	6	6	0	18	18	95^1	77	4	3.1	9.5	101	47%	.286
2017	DEB	A+	22	3	0	0	5	5	30^2	25	0	2.9	10.3	35	51%	.325
2020	TEX	MLB	25	2	2	0	33	0	35	35	5	3.7	8.9	35	45%	.308

Comparables: Shaun Anderson, Christian Garcia, Alex Meyer

This is almost certainly the case in other organizations too, but there's a large faction of the Rangers' most interesting pitchers whose recent stats are pretty sparse due to, what else, Tommy John surgery. Cody is one of those. He won the Rangers' Minor League Pitcher of the Year in 2017, and it appeared that he was on the train to Arlington, ETA 2020. Instead, he has only pitched a total of five innings since receiving the award, and while he hasn't pitched above High-A the Rangers added him to the 40-man roster this winter.

YEAR	TEAM	LVL	AGE	WHIP	ERA	DRA	WARP	MPH	FB%	WHF	CSP
2017	HIC	A	22	1.15	2.83	3.54	1.9				
2017	DEB	A+	22	1.14	2.05	3.79	0.5				
2020	TEX	MLB	25	1.43	4.84	4.73	0.2				

Hans Crouse RHP
Born: 09/15/98 Age: 21 Bats: L Throws: R
Height: 6'4" Weight: 180 Origin: Round 2, 2017 Draft (#66 overall)

YEAR	TEAM	LVL	AGE	W	L	SV	G	GS	IP	H	HR	BB/9	K/9	K	GB%	BABIP
2017	RNG	RK	18	0	0	0	10	6	20	7	1	3.2	13.5	30	60%	.176
2018	SPO	A-	19	5	1	0	8	8	38	25	2	2.6	11.1	47	36%	.253
2018	HIC	A	19	0	2	0	5	5	16^2	18	1	4.3	8.1	15	40%	.333
2019	HIC	A	20	6	1	0	19	19	87^2	86	12	2.0	7.8	76	34%	.297
2020	TEX	MLB	21	2	2	0	33	0	35	36	6	3.3	7.0	27	33%	.288

Comparables: Joe Ross, Nate Adcock, Mike Foltynewicz

In the bright light of day, the little distractions can collectively stipple over the silence, making it seem like everything is copacetic beneath the white-noise surface. The promise of a silent night is perpetually inviting, like an old high school flame or a deceased relative—never aging, the memory always conjuring their best version. But the impossible promise is built on a static of little sounds and interactions. When the sun melts into the soil and the world yawns and flutters its eyelashes and blithely gives way to the night, the truth can no longer be glossed over. The universe shuts up and that's when you hear the howls—distant at first, then closer, then just outside your window until you can hear the breathing between the howls, the hot breath of the predator, sniffing at first, then pawing the walls for cracks, the scraping and howling building to a chilling roar that your radio cannot drown out. The danger is outside, yes, but you know that one of these nights it will find a crack you missed. It will come for you, and all the noises in the world cannot scream it into submission, cannot save you from its hunger, cannot add even one more second to your life.

You close the book and look at the wall with your head cocked to one side as if to imply "was that really necessary?" You scrunch your face slightly. That wasn't about Hans Crouse at all.

The book shakes in your lap and you are certain that you hear the beast again, just behind you, in a nearly imperceptible whisper… *"Wasn't it?"*

YEAR	TEAM	LVL	AGE	WHIP	ERA	DRA	WARP	MPH	FB%	WHF	CSP
2017	RNG	RK	18	0.70	0.45	0.00	1.3				
2018	SPO	A-	19	0.95	2.37	2.18	1.4				
2018	HIC	A	19	1.56	2.70	5.31	0.0				
2019	HIC	A	20	1.20	4.41	5.12	0.1				
2020	TEX	MLB	21	1.40	4.98	4.99	0.1				

Taylor Hearn LHP

Born: 08/30/94 Age: 25 Bats: L Throws: L
Height: 6'5" Weight: 210 Origin: Round 5, 2015 Draft (#164 overall)

YEAR	TEAM	LVL	AGE	W	L	SV	G	GS	IP	H	HR	BB/9	K/9	K	GB%	BABIP
2017	BRD	A+	22	4	6	0	18	17	87^1	65	8	3.8	10.9	106	50%	.281
2018	ALT	AA	23	3	6	0	19	19	104	75	6	3.3	9.3	107	41%	.256
2018	FRI	AA	23	1	2	0	5	5	25	29	5	3.2	11.9	33	36%	.375
2019	NAS	AAA	24	1	3	0	4	4	20	14	3	4.5	11.7	26	29%	.262
2019	TEX	MLB	24	0	1	0	1	1	0^1	3	0	108.0	0.0	0	50%	.750
2020	TEX	MLB	25	0	0	0	2	2	5	6	1	4.3	5.1	3	37%	.281

Comparables: Eric Skoglund, Taylor Rogers, Sean Nolin

Hang out with enough philosophy or astronomy majors and you're sure to get a lecture about how time is elastic. You don't have to explain that to Hearn—his big-league debut on April 25 was the answer to this question: When is an outing simultaneously brief and eternal? Yes, Hearn lasted just one-third of an inning. On the other hand, he threw 39 pitches and faced eight batters, eventually exiting the game only to learn that he had tweaked his elbow—called a "minor" injury at the time. When does a "a few weeks" mean "five-plus months"? Alas, while time is elastic, elbows are not: It was later reported that Hearn had also suffered an elbow fracture. The big lefty should be ready for 2020 and should get a shot at cracking the big-league rotation at some point, but it's hard to call 2019 anything but a lost season, an eternity squeezed into the first act of a play that will inevitably feel brief in retrospect.

YEAR	TEAM	LVL	AGE	WHIP	ERA	DRA	WARP	MPH	FB%	WHF	CSP
2017	BRD	A+	22	1.17	4.12	3.88	1.4				
2018	ALT	AA	23	1.09	3.12	3.02	2.8				
2018	FRI	AA	23	1.52	5.04	5.68	-0.1				
2019	NAS	AAA	24	1.20	4.05	2.90	0.7				
2019	TEX	MLB	24	21.00	108.00	1.88	0.0	93.9	69.2	2.6	43.8
2020	TEX	MLB	25	1.58	5.98	5.59	0.0	93.6	70.9	2.6	44.8

Jimmy Herget RHP

Born: 09/09/93 Age: 26 Bats: R Throws: R
Height: 6'3" Weight: 170 Origin: Round 6, 2015 Draft (#175 overall)

YEAR	TEAM	LVL	AGE	W	L	SV	G	GS	IP	H	HR	BB/9	K/9	K	GB%	BABIP
2017	PEN	AA	23	1	3	16	24	0	29^2	22	1	3.6	13.3	44	32%	.323
2017	LOU	AAA	23	3	1	9	28	0	32^1	30	4	2.5	7.8	28	38%	.283
2018	LOU	AAA	24	1	3	0	50	0	59^2	59	5	3.2	9.8	65	36%	.327
2019	LOU	AAA	25	3	4	2	48	0	58^2	41	7	5.5	10.4	68	37%	.246
2019	CIN	MLB	25	0	0	0	5	0	6^1	8	2	4.3	0.0	0	22%	.286
2020	TEX	MLB	26	1	2	0	33	0	35	54	12	5.1	8.9	34	35%	.382

Comparables: Chandler Shepherd, Akeel Morris, Heath Hembree

Herget, a right-handed sidearmer who relies more on deception than stuff (though he sits around 93 mph, so he isn't without teeth), is going to have to prove he can handle lefties enough at the major-league level to be of greater use than in some specialist role. He'll need to do it affirmatively—and quickly—in order to survive, given the league's implementation of the three-batter minimum ahead of his rookie season. (He probably would've settled for a fruitcake or a simple "Welcome to the league, meat," y'all.) Herget's minor-league numbers suggest he could be up for the task.

YEAR	TEAM	LVL	AGE	WHIP	ERA	DRA	WARP	MPH	FB%	WHF	CSP
2017	PEN	AA	23	1.15	2.73	2.76	0.7				
2017	LOU	AAA	23	1.21	3.06	3.94	0.5				
2018	LOU	AAA	24	1.34	3.47	4.95	0.1				
2019	LOU	AAA	25	1.31	2.91	3.12	1.8				
2019	CIN	MLB	25	1.74	4.26	8.49	-0.2	95.0	50.7	8.4	42.5
2020	TEX	MLB	26	2.11	10.09	6.94	-0.7	94.6	51.6	8.6	43.2

Yohander Méndez LHP

Born: 01/17/95   Age: 25   Bats: L   Throws: L
Height: 6'5"   Weight: 200   Origin: International Free Agent, 2011

YEAR	TEAM	LVL	AGE	W	L	SV	G	GS	IP	H	HR	BB/9	K/9	K	GB%	BABIP
2017	FRI	AA	22	7	8	0	24	24	137^2	114	23	2.8	8.1	124	46%	.256
2017	TEX	MLB	22	0	1	0	7	0	12^1	13	3	2.2	5.1	7	37%	.263
2018	DEB	A+	23	1	2	0	5	5	31	29	3	1.7	7.8	27	36%	.306
2018	FRI	AA	23	1	1	0	6	6	33	33	6	2.7	8.7	32	32%	.300
2018	ROU	AAA	23	0	7	0	12	12	58^1	65	13	3.7	7.7	50	40%	.310
2018	TEX	MLB	23	2	2	0	8	5	27^2	28	4	4.9	5.9	18	40%	.286
2019	FRI	AA	24	0	0	1	4	0	7^1	5	1	7.4	7.4	6	30%	.182
2019	NAS	AAA	24	0	1	0	5	0	7^1	3	1	2.5	18.4	15	30%	.222
2019	TEX	MLB	24	1	0	0	3	0	4^2	4	2	9.6	15.4	8	25%	.333
2020	TEX	MLB	25	2	2	0	36	0	38	41	6	5.1	6.8	29	36%	.296

Comparables: Stephen Gonsalves, Chase De Jong, Keyvius Sampson

Méndez has largely played the part of Wile E. Coyote in recent years. Every time it seems like he's about to succeed, something awful happens. He loses control of his inside fastball and discovers that he is hovering over the Grand Canyon, or takes the brunt of an organizational message about behavior and gets sent to High-A, or tweaks his elbow and rides a rocket ship into a tunnel that was just right there. Eventually, one must start to wonder if the creators of the narrative are cruel; if baseball is just some divine version of Calvinball, and the rules are that this man was built to be an object of scorn. But Méndez willed himself back to the big leagues by September, and while the results were mixed, there was a new twist: he was touching 97 with his fastball while working in relief. If the bullpen is where he's destined to land in 2020, perhaps he'll finally get to relax and sit down to a nice roadrunner dinner.

YEAR	TEAM	LVL	AGE	WHIP	ERA	DRA	WARP	MPH	FB%	WHF	CSP
2017	FRI	AA	22	1.14	3.79	4.07	1.8				
2017	TEX	MLB	22	1.30	5.11	7.67	-0.3	94.4	60.7	10	46.7
2018	DEB	A+	23	1.13	3.48	4.33	0.4				
2018	FRI	AA	23	1.30	4.91	4.82	0.2				
2018	ROU	AAA	23	1.53	5.25	6.19	-0.4				
2018	TEX	MLB	23	1.55	5.53	7.02	-0.6	94.6	59.9	9.6	48.3
2019	FRI	AA	24	1.50	1.23	4.39	0.0				
2019	NAS	AAA	24	0.68	4.91	1.06	0.4				
2019	TEX	MLB	24	1.93	5.79	4.81	0.0	95.4	41	13	35.8
2020	TEX	MLB	25	1.62	5.81	5.35	-0.1	94.4	58.3	10.5	43.7

Cole Ragans   LHP

Born: 12/12/97   Age: 22   Bats: L   Throws: L
Height: 6'4"   Weight: 190   Origin: Round 1, 2016 Draft (#30 overall)

YEAR	TEAM	LVL	AGE	W	L	SV	G	GS	IP	H	HR	BB/9	K/9	K	GB%	BABIP
2017	SPO	A-	19	3	2	0	13	13	57^1	50	5	5.5	13.7	87	42%	.369
2020	TEX	MLB	22	2	2	0	33	0	35	36	6	4.2	9.3	36	38%	.312

Comparables: Miguel Castro, Drew Anderson, Jake Brigham

Ragans is another of the Rangers' impressive all-Tommy-John-prospects rotation. In fact, he's the grizzled veteran of the bunch, having now undergone the procedure twice. When he's been able to stay healthy, he's been impressive, earning comparisons in his first spring training to another crafty left-hander named Cole (Hamels). 2020 is going to be a pivotal year for Ragans after missing so much action. The team isn't going to rush him through the system just to make up for lost time, but they will indubitably be watching closely to see how much rust has accumulated in the time off, and how his body responds to being in a competitive setting again after so long living in a red t-shirt. He's still just 21, but he does need to stay healthy.

YEAR	TEAM	LVL	AGE	WHIP	ERA	DRA	WARP	MPH	FB%	WHF	CSP
2017	SPO	A-	19	1.48	3.61	3.71	1.1				
2020	TEX	MLB	22	1.48	5.14	5.11	0.0				

Alex Speas RHP

Born: 03/04/98 Age: 22 Bats: R Throws: R
Height: 6'4" Weight: 180 Origin: Round 2, 2016 Draft (#63 overall)

YEAR	TEAM	LVL	AGE	W	L	SV	G	GS	IP	H	HR	BB/9	K/9	K	GB%	BABIP
2017	SPO	A-	19	1	6	1	16	7	33²	29	5	6.7	12.0	45	42%	.282
2018	HIC	A	20	2	0	6	20	0	28²	16	1	6.6	15.4	49	56%	.283
2020	TEX	MLB	22	2	2	0	33	0	35	36	6	4.5	10.3	40	41%	.324

Comparables: Darwinzon Hernandez, Brock Burke, Drew Anderson

Let's start with the bad news for Speas: 1. He has pitched in two games (one inning) since June 11, 2018, having undergone Tommy John surgery, because how else would you expect that phrase to end? It would be a much more interesting story to say that he had taken time off to study under a farce guru who promised to teach the lad how to hypnotize dolphins, in case he was ever on a cruise ship and a dolphin leapt aboard and began haranguing the passengers, but Speas discovered the grift and brought the fraud to justice. Heck of a story; most interesting player in the game, instantly. But no, it was just the same crappy surgery that steals years from pitchers with brutal regularity. 2. His name sounds like a combination of "soup" and "peas", like if you meant to say "pea soup" but you were distracted thinking about the logistics of how exactly the dolphin would go about haranguing passengers anyway, and your brain just slung the words out of your mouth carelessly. "Speeeaas". The good news? Dude is throwing 102mph in his side sessions now and might be a big-leaguer before the season is over.

YEAR	TEAM	LVL	AGE	WHIP	ERA	DRA	WARP	MPH	FB%	WHF	CSP
2017	SPO	A-	19	1.60	6.15	4.28	0.3				
2018	HIC	A	20	1.29	2.20	2.67	0.7				
2020	TEX	MLB	22	1.52	5.29	5.20	0.0				

Ricky Vanasco RHP

Born: 10/13/98 Age: 21 Bats: R Throws: R
Height: 6'3" Weight: 180 Origin: Round 15, 2017 Draft (#464 overall)

YEAR	TEAM	LVL	AGE	W	L	SV	G	GS	IP	H	HR	BB/9	K/9	K	GB%	BABIP
2017	RNG	RK	18	0	1	0	10	0	9	8	0	5.0	16.0	16	47%	.421
2018	RNG	RK	19	3	3	0	7	3	24²	25	1	4.7	9.1	25	48%	.393
2019	SPO	A-	20	3	1	0	9	9	39	23	2	5.1	13.6	59	51%	.292
2019	HIC	A	20	0	0	0	2	2	10²	5	0	2.5	13.5	16	47%	.263
2020	TEX	MLB	21	2	2	0	33	0	35	35	5	3.8	10.9	42	44%	.328

Comparables: Dylan Cease, Domingo Germán, Neftalí Feliz

If you're wondering "who the heck is Ricky Vanasco?" you're not alone. Unless you work for the Rangers, in which case, hoooo boy are you ever alone, and also you should probably update your resumé, because he went from relative unknown to organizational hot gossip in a very short amount of time. His previous anonymity was less to do with futility and more with bad luck—the 15th-round pick's first season in pro ball ended when catcher Sam Huff hit him in the back of the head while attempting to throw out a would-be base thief. After a long concussion recovery, Vanasco missed the end of the 2018 season with an elbow injury that did not require surgery. So imagine everyone's surprise when the 20-year-old took short-season Spokane by storm, then didn't miss a beat when he was promoted to Low-A. The helium year didn't just occur from being healthy; there was also the added benefit of his fastball hopping up into the mid-to-high 90s. It will be fascinating to see how aggressive the Rangers are in promoting him through the system.

YEAR	TEAM	LVL	AGE	WHIP	ERA	DRA	WARP	MPH	FB%	WHF	CSP
2017	RNG	RK	18	1.44	0.00	2.70	0.3				
2018	RNG	RK	19	1.54	4.38	6.31	-0.1				
2019	SPO	A-	20	1.15	1.85	3.10	1.0				
2019	HIC	A	20	0.75	1.69	2.70	0.3				
2020	TEX	MLB	21	1.41	4.68	4.73	0.2				

Cole Winn   RHP

Born: 11/25/99   Age: 20   Bats: R   Throws: R
Height: 6'2"   Weight: 190   Origin: Round 1, 2018 Draft (#15 overall)

YEAR	TEAM	LVL	AGE	W	L	SV	G	GS	IP	H	HR	BB/9	K/9	K	GB%	BABIP
2019	HIC	A	19	4	4	0	18	18	68^2	59	5	5.1	8.5	65	48%	.290
2020	TEX	MLB	20	2	2	0	33	0	35	35	6	4.1	6.7	26	44%	.280

Comparables: Luke Jackson, Tyler Chatwood, Mauricio Cabrera

Everybody fails; that's the one lesson that the sport is better at teaching than any other. But not everyone finds the right levers to steady the ship before being dashed on the rocks. Winn spent the early part of 2019 taking on water at Low-A Hickory following his 2018 post-draft hiatus from pitching, which is part of the Rangers' de-load program. But as the season progressed, the starboard-side slinger gradually began weathering the storms a little better, using his four-pitch mix with increasing effectiveness. It's also important to remember that Winn was only 19 last season. At that age, most guys are still navigating rookie or short-season ball, and he was figuring it out in deeper waters. There's still a lot of sea to explore before Winn pulls into the big leagues, but…hey, we're going to just let you choose your own pun-adventure here. Circle one: "something something learn from the stars." / "something something prove he can Winn."

YEAR	TEAM	LVL	AGE	WHIP	ERA	DRA	WARP	MPH	FB%	WHF	CSP
2019	HIC	A	19	1.43	4.46	5.47	-0.2				
2020	TEX	MLB	20	1.45	4.95	4.94	0.1				

LINEOUTS

Hitters

HITTER	POS	TEAM	LVL	AGE	PA	R	2B	3B	HR	RBI	BB	K	SB	CS	AVG/OBP/SLG	DRC+	WARP
Tim Federowicz	C	COH	AAA	31	103	7	6	0	2	13	11	23	0	0	.278/.353/.411	98	0.5
	C	TEX	MLB	31	83	6	2	0	4	7	5	31	1	0	.160/.213/.347	69	0.1
	C	NAS	AAA	31	63	5	0	0	1	8	4	16	0	0	.140/.190/.193	26	-0.1
Logan Forsythe	INF	TEX	MLB	32	367	38	17	1	7	39	44	100	2	0	.227/.325/.353	87	0.5
Adolis Garcia	OF	MEM	AAA	26	529	96	22	6	32	96	22	159	14	10	.253/.301/.517	91	2.4
Pedro Gonzalez	OF	HIC	A	21	459	69	13	5	23	67	39	129	14	6	.248/.317/.471	119	1.6
Julio Pablo Martinez	OF	HIC	A	23	44	7	1	1	1	5	3	12	4	1	.250/.295/.400	112	0.0
	OF	DEB	A+	23	456	59	21	4	14	58	39	144	28	12	.248/.319/.423	111	1.6
Blake Swihart	LF	RNO	AAA	27	122	20	2	1	6	22	15	31	0	1	.189/.287/.396	68	-0.4
	LF	BOS	MLB	27	29	4	1	0	1	4	2	7	0	0	.231/.310/.385	98	0.0
	LF	ARI	MLB	27	70	9	0	0	3	9	4	29	0	0	.136/.186/.273	49	-0.2

Maximo Acosta has opened a few eyes in his short amount of time in the organization. Just 17, he's a bit further away from than some of the other Rangers' infield prospects, but it wouldn't be a major surprise if he ends up being the best among them. ⓧ Between Jeff Mathis and **Tim Federowicz**, last year's Rangers employed two of the seven worst hitting catchers in the majors dating back to the 2011 season. Jon Daniels should charge a small fee to pick people's HACKING MASS backstops for them. ⓧ At the onset of the season, it appeared that **Logan Forsythe** was on the Hunter Pence plan for career rejuvenation in Texas. Both had markedly worse second halves — Pence due to injury, and Forsythe due to regression (and then injury). ⓧ All strikeouts and no walks make **Adolis García** a dull prospect. All strikeouts and no walks make Adolis García a dull prospect. All strikeouts and no walks make Adolis García a dull prospect.... ⓧ Much like your rich uncle who never fixes anything himself, **Pedro Gonzalez** has all the tools—you just haven't ever seen him use them. ⓧ It took until August for the Rangers to trade for enough international slot money to pay **Bayron Lora**'s $3.9 million bonus, but he's officially in Rangers gear now. Big gear. Some of the biggest gear they have, in fact, as the 16-year-old is listed at 6-foot-4, 200 pounds. ⓧ The Rangers hoped that **Julio Pablo Martinez** would be the next Cuban sensation when they signed him for $2.8 million in 2018. With 156 strikeouts in 447 at-bats in 2019 there seemed to be a Cuban *missing* crisis (get it?!), though he did finish the season strong. ⓧ In early September 2019, the Hubble Telescope captured stunning images of the star known as NGC 2371/2 dying in deep space. Scientists initially confused the image with that of former catching prospect **Blake Swihart**. ⓧ **Davis Wendzel** was Big 12 co-Player of the Year, then got drafted by the same organization that drafted the other guy (Josh Jung). Both play third base, but Wendzel is generally considered to be more versatile, and might end up as a Ben Zobrist-type.

Texas Rangers 2020

Pitchers

PITCHER	TEAM	LVL	AGE	W	L	SV	G	GS	IP	H	HR	BB/9	K/9	K	GB%	WHIP	ERA	DRA	WARP
Joe Barlow	DEB	A+	23	4	0	4	17	0	23^2	10	1	5.7	16.7	44	32%	1.06	0.38	2.16	0.7
	FRI	AA	23	1	1	0	13	0	16	6	1	3.4	15.2	27	42%	0.75	1.12	2.01	0.5
	NAS	AAA	23	1	1	0	19	0	17^1	23	1	10.9	11.4	22	37%	2.54	8.83	8.07	-0.3
Jesse Biddle	TEX	MLB	27	0	0	0	4	0	5^1	4	2	8.4	11.8	7	69%	1.69	11.81	8.16	-0.2
	SEA	MLB	27	0	0	0	11	0	11	20	2	5.7	6.5	8	46%	2.45	9.82	8.53	-0.4
	ATL	MLB	27	0	1	0	15	0	11^2	18	1	7.7	8.5	11	44%	2.40	5.40	5.21	0.0
Tim Dillard	NAS	AAA	35	9	9	0	33	21	153^1	169	16	2.2	6.0	103	55%	1.34	4.75	4.41	3.3
Kyle Dowdy	AKR	AA	26	1	1	0	7	3	29	25	2	3.4	8.4	27	41%	1.24	2.48	5.01	-0.1
	NAS	AAA	26	1	1	0	8	1	12^1	13	0	7.3	8.0	11	50%	1.86	6.57	4.87	0.2
	TEX	MLB	26	2	1	0	13	1	22^1	26	4	7.3	6.9	17	45%	1.97	7.25	6.68	-0.3
Demarcus Evans	DEB	A+	22	4	0	6	17	0	22^1	9	0	6.9	16.1	40	55%	1.16	0.81	3.02	0.4
	FRI	AA	22	2	0	6	30	0	37^2	14	2	5.3	14.3	60	37%	0.96	0.96	2.36	1.0
Luke Farrell	FRI	AA	28	0	0	0	5	0	8^2	2	0	4.2	12.5	12	43%	0.69	1.04	2.28	0.2
	TEX	MLB	28	1	0	0	9	1	13^1	6	3	2.0	8.1	12	27%	0.68	2.70	5.15	0.0
Brian Flynn	OMA	AAA	29	4	4	0	11	5	43^1	47	7	3.7	8.7	42	44%	1.50	4.78	4.08	1.0
	KCA	MLB	29	2	2	0	11	1	29^1	38	2	5.2	6.8	22	46%	1.88	5.22	8.32	-0.9
Ian Gibaut	DUR	AAA	25	1	0	4	11	1	10^1	7	0	8.7	13.9	16	41%	1.65	3.48	4.33	0.2
	TBA	MLB	25	0	0	0	1	0	2	1	0	9.0	9.0	2	20%	1.50	9.00	6.29	0.0
	TEX	MLB	25	1	1	0	9	0	12^1	11	1	5.8	10.2	14	50%	1.54	5.11	4.35	0.1
Jeanmar Gomez	TEX	MLB	31	1	0	0	16	0	15^1	23	2	3.5	5.9	10	55%	1.89	8.22	5.54	0.0
Taylor Guerrieri	NAS	AAA	26	1	3	0	23	2	36^1	36	1	3.7	9.7	39	58%	1.40	3.47	3.05	1.1
	TEX	MLB	26	0	0	0	20	0	26^1	26	3	7.5	9.2	27	56%	1.82	5.81	5.97	-0.2
Ronny Henriquez	HIC	A	19	6	6	0	21	19	82	91	6	3.0	10.9	99	39%	1.44	4.50	5.91	-0.7
Jonathan Hernandez	FRI	AA	22	5	9	0	22	16	96	100	11	3.6	8.9	95	48%	1.44	5.16	5.72	-1.0
	TEX	MLB	22	2	1	0	9	2	16^2	14	3	7.0	10.3	19	52%	1.62	4.32	5.05	0.1
Wei-Chieh Huang	FRI	AA	25	1	0	0	6	1	9^2	7	2	1.9	13.0	14	24%	0.93	1.86	3.25	0.2
	NAS	AAA	25	1	2	0	18	3	31	24	5	7.3	12.2	42	29%	1.58	6.10	4.30	0.6
	TEX	MLB	25	0	0	0	4	0	5^2	8	0	7.9	3.2	2	42%	2.29	3.18	5.11	0.0
Tyler Phillips	DEB	A+	21	2	2	0	6	6	37^2	28	1	1.4	6.7	28	57%	0.90	1.19	3.46	0.7
	FRI	AA	21	7	9	0	18	16	93^1	95	15	1.9	7.1	74	52%	1.23	4.72	5.29	-0.4
Adrian Sampson	TEX	MLB	27	6	8	0	35	15	125^1	156	29	2.6	7.3	101	42%	1.53	5.89	7.49	-2.5
Jeffrey Springs	NAS	AAA	26	3	0	0	6	0	7	6	1	0.0	15.4	12	50%	0.86	3.86	1.59	0.3
	TEX	MLB	26	4	1	0	25	0	32^1	38	4	6.4	8.9	32	25%	1.89	6.40	7.98	-0.9

A lot of folks were starting to wonder if **Joe Barlow** was going to get a call-up in 2019. Instead, his struggles with control returned when he got to Nashville. **Jesse Biddle** was once famous for spinning a curveball that you could *hear* on the way to the plate. Now it's surprising whenever you hear he's on a 25-man roster. ⚾ You probably know **Tim Dillard** more for his social media presence than his on-field performance, but he bailed out the Nashville Sounds on multiple occasions when they desperately needed innings in 2019. Texas rewarded him with a flight to Arlington—he wasn't added to the big-league roster, but he did some sideline reporting, some player interviews, and ran in the Dot Race. ⚾ **Kyle Dowdy** should perhaps rebrand as BByle Dowdy, given that his unsightly 16 percent walk rate eclipsed his meager 15 percent strikeout rate in 22 1/3 big-league innings. ⚾ The Rangers decided that **Demarcus Evans** had too good a 2019 to be left vulnerable in the Rule 5 draft. If his 2020 is anything like his 2019, he'll pitch in the big leagues anyway (just probably not on Opening Day). ⚾ **Luke Farrell** spent most of 2019 recovering from a broken jaw he sustained in spring training when he was hit with a nasty line drive. Getting back to the big leagues at all was a success; the impressive numbers were a bonus. ⚾ Fun fact: **Brian Flynn** started one game for the Royals in 2019, and it was shorter than eight of his 10 relief appearances. Maybe it wasn't fun for Flynn. ⚾ Which number is higher: career big-league innings for **Ian Gibaut** through 2019 (14 1/3) or times he has had to politely pretend to chuckle at references to 1990s jeans brand Marithé + François Girbaud? We bet it's close. ⚾ In a small sample of innings, **Jeanmar Gómez** gave up a large sample of runs. He did manage to keep the ball on the ground, which might grant him a minor-league deal at some point. ⚾ **Taylor Guerrieri**: his pitches :: baseball writers : vowels in his last name. (a basic but imprecise idea of where they're going). Still, his curveball is good enough that he'll pitch somewhere in 2020. ⚾ It's a safe bet to say **Ronny Henriquez** will eventually end up in the bullpen, but perhaps only because it's always a safe bet to say that; a lot of pitchers end up there. To his credit, he skipped straight from the DSL to Low-A Hickory and held his own pretty well as a 19-year-old. ⚾ It's fun to play this game, so here: in **Jonathan Hernández**' big-league debut, he faced Albert Pujols and the game was won on a Hunter Pence walk-off single. For now that's not a super-fun fact, so it's up to Hernandez to stick around long enough to let it age into a fine vintage fun fact. ⚾ Speaking of debuts, **Wei-Chieh Huang** was another of the 13 pitchers to make their big-league debut with the Rangers in 2019. Unlucky numbers aren't real, but tell that to those guys, who had a combined ERA of 6.02. ⚾ After being named the Rangers' 2018 Minor League pitcher of the year, **Tyler Phillips** dominated again at High-A, then struggled when he got to Double-A. That doesn't really scream "ready for a full season in the majors," but the Rangers went ahead and added him to the 40-man roster to protect him from the Rule 5 draft anyway. ⚾ **Adrian Sampson** established himself as one of baseball's premier grumps when he bickered with the A's about bat flips, and one of baseball's more creative grumps when he stepped on Ramón Laureano's bat. Not cool, but definitely funny. He'll be playing in Korea in 2020. ⚾ **Jeffrey Springs** has done just that—he was not a highly-lauded prospect out of college, but his double-plus changeup has taken him much further than most would have expected. ⑰ If you read last year's essay, the demise of the Rangers' "de-load" program is probably not a huge surprise to you. **Owen White** is one of the pitchers for whom the program did not prevent a Tommy John surgery. As a result (of both the program and the surgery, which was done in May of 2019), the second-round pick from the 2018 draft still hasn't thrown a single pitch in his professional career, and likely won't until two full years after being drafted.

Rangers Prospects

The State of the System

Shockingly, the Rangers are once again loaded with low minors, high upside talent. As usual, Hickory and Down East will be must-see in 2020.

The Top Ten

─────── ★ ★ ★ *2020 Top 101 Prospect* **#37** ★ ★ ★ ───────

1
Leody Taveras OF   OFP: 60   ETA: 2020
Born: 09/08/98 Age: 21 Bats: B Throws: R Height: 6'1" Weight: 171
Origin: International Free Agent, 2015

The Report: Movement quality, general athleticism, premium baseball instincts, and an athlete's build give Taveras one of the most "pleasing to the eye" games in minor-league baseball. Taveras bursts into action at the plate or in the field, showing plus bat speed or quick 0-100 closing speed on fly balls. Taveras makes quick reads and decisions on the bases or the grass, and his plus-plus athleticism takes care of the rest of the job.

His impressive bat speed generates plus raw power, although an inconsistent plan of attack at the plate keeps him from tapping into it. Despite that, he generally makes good contact and has enough pitch recognition and patience for a respectable OBP-first profile with flashes of impact upside. If he doesn't tap into it, he could see seasons on offense somewhere in between Leonys Martin and Ender Inciarte, but if he does make the needed adjustment he could provide above-average production with the bat. The right-handed swing has lagged behind the left, but Taveras is making good adjustments with tracking the lefty breaking ball and started to show a similar power profile from both sides.

He is a plus runner who makes excellent reads, takes good routes, and flashes an above-average arm. Taveras makes the kind of 50/50 plays that many center fielders require max effort to get to without breaking into a full sprint due to quick jumps and seemingly instant acceleration.

Overall, Taveras profiles as an above-average regular with impact defensive value in center field and an AVG/OBP profile in the lineup. There's significant upside in his power projection, and if he can just tap into some of it, he could be a plus regular.

Variance: Medium. There's a high floor with the speed/glove up the middle, but the ultimate outcome in the bat could put Taveras anywhere from bench outfielder to All-Star.

Ben Carsley's Fantasy Take: I might need to go into Witness Protection if Jeff reads this, but I think Taveras is a substantially better real life prospect than fantasy prospect. The speed is nice of course, as is the fact that Taveras' glove should keep him in the lineup. But the power is mostly projection at this point, and I'm not a big believer in his ability to hit from the right. His upside remains very attractive, and because of the speed his floor is high enough that Taveras is definitely a top-101 dude. I'm just not betting on fantasy stardom, though I'll be pleasantly surprised if he makes it happen.

★ ★ ★ *2020 Top 101 Prospect* #70 ★ ★ ★

2 **Josh Jung** 3B OFP: 60 ETA: 2022
Born: 02/12/98 Age: 22 Bats: R Throws: R Height: 6'2" Weight: 215
Origin: Round 1, 2019 Draft (#8 overall)

The Report: The hit tool is explosive. Jung's well-muscled build generates impact bat speed and he can cover any portion of the zone. Batting practice sees him scorching hard contact pull-side or up the middle from a compact swing. The righty has the physical markers for a plus hit tool at the major league level, and it wouldn't take much to get him there. Unfortunately his approach is often tailored for opposite field contact as he tries to go with the ball instead of focusing on doing damage. He rarely gets on plane with the ball, even on inside pitches, and as such he sees a significant number of low line drives and ground balls. Jung has plus raw power and possibly could tap into more if there was intent to do damage when he swings. A "go with the ball" mentality is wasted on someone with Jung's physical abilities. The former Raider will also need to iron out some issues with his ability to pick up spin, specifically low and outside breakers.

Defensively, Jung flashes good hands and has an above-average arm, but he attacks the ball standing almost straight up and the change in eye height going to meet the ball can cause some predictable miscues. The physical traits suggest he should be able to provide average value at the hot corner with some adjustments to how he approaches groundballs.

Jung should find himself fitting on a major league team as a regular at third where his batting average, mid-teens home run power, and average glove will make him a clear contributor. Jung's hit tool and plus raw power give him significant upside if he changes his approach and improves his spin recognition.

Variance: Medium. Much like with Taveras, the ultimate power output will shape the profile, as the hit tool and glove at third give Jung a likely major league future of some sort.

Ben Carsley's Fantasy Take: Honestly, I can't be trusted with this profile. Hit tool-first third baseman who go the other way and have potential power? Be still, my heavily-taxed heart. Jung should move fast given his pedigree as a first-round college bat and his advanced approach at the plate, which means I'm going to push for him to rank as a top-50ish dynasty league prospect already. If it all really clicks, I think he could get most of the way to a Justin Turner-esque fantasy profile. We'll see how good Bret, Mark and co. are at tempering my excitement.

───── ★ ★ ★ *2020 Top 101 Prospect* **#74** ★ ★ ★ ─────

3 Nick Solak   IF   OFP: 55   ETA: 2019
Born: 01/11/95   Age: 25   Bats: R   Throws: R   Height: 5'11"   Weight: 190
Origin: Round 2, 2016 Draft (#62 overall)

The Report: We never really had much doubt Nick Solak would hit, even going back two orgs ago to his time with the Yankees. The term "professional hitter" was all but invented for him. That usually implies something about the player's defense, and here, yeah I mean it fits. Solak played second base primarily in the minors, but he was never all that good there, and his arm is probably a little short for third. He has some corner outfield experience as well, so you have options to get his bat in the lineup. The Rangers will want to, because Solak has added power year-over-year, and while his 31 homers at three levels this year is too rich to project for him in the majors, something like .280 with low-20s bombs is certainly in play now. He's gotten to his power without lengthening his compact swing, and he gets on-base at a good clip and can run well. He's not quite the the Hubie Brooks "F to a C+" wherever you put him, but C- is a passing grade when you hit like Solak.

Variance: Low. He's already conquered the upper minors and had a solid major league cup of coffee. He's barely eligible for this list, and we have little doubt he will hit enough to outpace the defensive issues, even if they will also limit his upside.

Ben Carsley's Fantasy Take: Seriously, what is it with the Rangers and small, positionless dudes who can rake? I think the biggest danger with Solak is that his glove will keep him off the field more than we'd care for, making him a dude who earns more like 400 at-bats a year than 600 when the Rangers are competitive. But no one doubts that he can hit, he's ready to play now, and he should offer multi-position eligibility for a bit. It's a weird-ass fantasy profile to be sure, but also a very intriguing one.

4 Joe Palumbo   LHP   OFP: 60   ETA: 2019
Born: 10/26/94   Age: 25   Bats: L   Throws: L   Height: 6'1"   Weight: 168
Origin: Round 30, 2013 Draft (#910 overall)

The Report: It's hard to find a lefty with a better three-pitch mix in the minors than Joe Palumbo. On good nights he flashes a mid-90s high-spin four-seamer, a plus two-plane curveball, and a plus changeup with both tumble and fade. He throws enough strikes and misses plenty of bats, but unfortunately inconsistency can ruin otherwise stellar outings. Palumbo's fastball command comes and goes at the best of times, which can put him into problem counts too often. His curveball can at times flatten out and get hammered when left in the zone. Even on bad nights he will still miss bats thanks to his changeup, which has become a consistent offering, but hitters can sit fastball and do damage.

Palmubo is only a season and change removed from coming back from Tommy John surgery, so it's possible that his command inconsistencies will lessen with a bit more time. Regardless, it creates the risk that he won't find enough command or consistency to stick in a rotation, but will be forced into a pen role.

As it is, Palumbo's stuff still warrants a projection as middle-of-the-rotation arm, but with significant risk that he ends up in the bullpen before long. Conversely, he also has one of the higher upsides in the Rangers system, and could end up as a high-end third starter if he can iron out the command.

Variance: High. The command will dictate the eventual role here, and there are health and durability red flags as well.

Ben Carsley's Fantasy Take: Sub out "curveball" for "slider" above and it would sure feel like you were reading an Eduardo Rodriguez scouting report, no? That's the type of upside Palumbo possesses; a good fantasy SP4/5 who racks up strikeouts, but who doesn't always perform consistently from year-to-year (or, uh, start-to-start, or inning-to-inning). I'd like Palumbo more were he in an organization with a better track record of developing pitching, but even so he's a borderline top-101 guy thanks to his proximity.

5. Sam Huff   C   OFP: 55   ETA: 2022
Born: 01/14/98   Age: 22   Bats: R   Throws: R   Height: 6'4"   Weight: 230
Origin: Round 7, 2016 Draft (#219 overall)

The Report: Without a doubt the highest riser in the Rangers system this year, Huff went from someone on some people's radars to the middle of everyone's. After a good year in Hickory, Huff repeated his results at both A-ball levels. He is definitely a bat-first catcher, with plus power and a solid hit tool. One thing holding Huff back offensively is his decision making at the dish; better pitch recognition and a more patient approach is something he'll want to work on going forward.

Huff's defense behind the plate isn't awe inspiring, but does show good athleticism and a willingness to hustle and improve. Catchers are notoriously slow-developing players, but Huff has accelerated his development and become the top backstop in the Texas system. With his size there will always be questions about whether his long term future is in the crouch or at, say, first base. For now, Huff's abilities and skills can keep him catching without being a defensive liability. With no one blocking Huff on the depth chart, his performance next season and beyond is the only thing limiting his future.

Variance: High. Catchers, man. They're always a little hard to predict. In Huff's case the questions come about whether he can hold up behind the plate long term. His future changes if he is forced into a corner infield or outfield position. Time will tell, but it's something to keep in mind.

Ben Carsley's Fantasy Take: I know this might not be a popular take, but I'm letting others go all-in on Huff while I watch from a distance. He's far from a lock to stay at catcher, and even if he does manage to stay behind the plate for a bit, then we get to worry about the horrendous track record for fantasy catching prospects at large. Yes, there's a chance he's Mitch Garver, but there's also a chance he's…Tom Murphy? Jacob Nottingham? Fancy Dog Zack Collins? Huff should be owned in leagues that roster 200-plus prospects, but odds are he'll be showing up on some dynasty top-100 lists this winter, and I won't agree with those rankings.

6. Hans Crouse   RHP   OFP: 55   ETA: 2022
Born: 09/15/98   Age: 21   Bats: L   Throws: R   Height: 6'4"   Weight: 180
Origin: Round 2, 2017 Draft (#66 overall)

The Report: Crouse has a lot of the traits you look for in a big-time pitcher. He's got the height and frame typically desired, as well as a competitive fire that often manifests itself visibly on the field. Not only is it evident in how he owns the mound during his starts, or in his reactions after a big out, but Crouse pitched roughly the last half of this season with a bone spur in his elbow and performed admirably anyway.

It's not just empty bluster on the mound, either. Crouse has a pair of pitches that project plus in a fastball that sits in the mid 90s and a low-80s curve that he manipulates and is good for plenty of swings and misses. There is also a considerable amount he has to improve on, and there are aspects to the profile that will be of concern until they aren't, so to speak. The command isn't a strength at this point, and there's a lot of violence in the delivery, so a starting outcome is far from a guarantee. His current injury will be taken care of in the offseason, but elbow issues are always worrisome. He hasn't really had a third pitch declare itself yet, either. The high-80s change is pretty firm but shows enough fade that it holds some promise, though he doesn't use it much at present.

Variance: Medium. A lot of what is outlined in the report points to significant reliever risk, but the stuff and overall package is enough to be comfortable projecting a productive big leaguer of some kind.

Ben Carsley's Fantasy Take: Crouse belongs near the top of that big, mushy group of 20-or-so potential mid-rotation starters who generally just make the tail end or barely miss our top-101 dynasty list every season. He's got size and stuff on his side, but organizational weakness and reliever risk against him. That third pitch will be pretty important for his fantasy value, so keep an eye on his development in shallow leagues; in deeper ones, he's rightfully already owned.

7 Brock Burke   LHP   OFP: 50   ETA: 2019
Born: 08/04/96 Age: 23 Bats: L Throws: L Height: 6'4" Weight: 180
Origin: Round 3, 2014 Draft (#96 overall)

The Report: A solid three-pitch mix helped the big lefty carve up the Texas League when he was healthy. Burke features a good fastball that sat low 90s but could pop higher on occasion, a firm changeup in the low 80s with good sink, and a curveball that wasn't fully developed, but had enough consistent shape and command that Double-A hitters weren't able to handle it. By the end of the season, he had added a slider which became his primary breaking pitch. Part of that is due to the slider revolution across the game and part of it was Burke's blister issues, which made the curve a less than ideal option. Burke having the ability to throw both only helps him, assuming he can find a way to throw the curve without pain. His development is still ongoing, but when right Burke has shown the tools and knowledge to get hitters back into the dugout, and given the dearth of starting pitching options in Texas at the moment, he may have spent his last year in the minors.

Variance: High. The injury factor is the big player here; with blister and shoulder issues already on the board, Burke is a high risk to spend time on the injured list going forward. If those issues are non-factors, Burke could pitch for a decade and maybe bump up a half grade on the OFP. Until he shows major league durability, Burke's projection remains somewhat cloudy.

Ben Carsley's Fantasy Take: Nope. Between the lack of upside, the injury risk and this org's track record, I'm all set. You should be too.

8 Sherten Apostel   3B   OFP: 55   ETA: 2022
Born: 03/11/99 Age: 21 Bats: R Throws: R Height: 6'4" Weight: 200
Origin: International Free Agent, 2018

The Report: Apostel has big tools, and he's translated enough of them into on-field performance to have gotten to the Carolina League as a 20-year-old. He has a well-filled out, strong and athletic frame. The two notable tools for the Curaçaoan are big power and an exceptional arm. The present hit tool could inspire a wide range of opinions depending on what day you see him. There is plus bat speed and Apostel makes very satisfying contact when he squares it up. He will whiff a fair bit though, which is not a surprise given the long levers and corresponding length in his swing. That contributes to a high strikeout rate at present, but he also has excellent plate discipline. The approach can border on passiveness though, and put him behind in counts as often as it gets him ahead. This is obviously beneficial to him when he gets a good pitch in a hitter's count, but the early selectivity can dig a hole which accounts for some of the strikeouts.

Apostel's offensive profile is ideal for third base, but there are already questions about whether he'll stick at the hot corner long term. I think he's fine there at present. While he isn't the smoothest or most natural-looking defender, his range, instincts, and first step are good enough. Still, he's not going to get any quicker, and if he fills out any more he might be a first baseman.

Variance: High. There's development that needs to happen with the hit tool and he'll probably need to sharpen up his defense as well, but time is on his side. A move to first base would put significant pressure on the bat, though.

Ben Carsley's Fantasy Take: Apostel already started to get some buzz in dynasty leagues last season, and it's easy to see why. I wish we could be slightly more confident in his ability to stay at third long term, but Apostel has the power and approach required to potentially be fantasy-relevant even if he does move to the cold corner. He should be owned in any league that rosters 125-plus prospects. If you're the type who bases your team name off your roster, Apostel is arguably a top-2 dude.

9. Cole Winn   RHP   OFP: 55   ETA: 2022
Born: 11/25/99   Age: 20   Bats: R   Throws: R   Height: 6'2"   Weight: 190
Origin: Round 1, 2018 Draft (#15 overall)

The Report: As a first-round prep arm receiving plaudits for his command, Winn came out of last year's draft saddled with high expectations. Early struggles following this year's aggressive assignment to full-season ball have seen him slip in some quarters, but he finished the campaign well and will enter next season as a strong bounceback candidate. The command didn't live up to expectations early on, but it improved as time went on and projects as potential plus with his clean and repeatable delivery. Winn sits mid 90s with the heater, flashing life up in the zone where it can be a swing-and-miss offering. There is an easy plus fastball here when he commands it. The curveball is his best secondary and also projects plus. The hook is a high-70s, 12-to-6 breaker coming with good bite that he can spot for strikes or put away hitters out of the zone. The low-80s slider and mid-80s change flash above-average, and it certainly looks like there is a legitimate four-pitch mix developing.

Variance: Medium. Risk is inherent with prep arms and Winn didn't set the world on fire in his debut season. There aren't many red flags here though, and what he may lack in upside he should make up for in polish.

Ben Carsley's Fantasy Take: Although they're very different pitchers, Winn doesn't rank too differently than Crouse will in my eyes. He lacks some of Crouse's upside, but he's also a safer bet to remain a starter long-term. At a certain point, this really just comes down to your preference in pitcher profile.

Texas Rangers 2020

10 **Bubba Thompson** OF OFP: 50 ETA: 2022
Born: 06/09/98 Age: 22 Bats: R Throws: R Height: 6'1" Weight: 180
Origin: Round 1, 2017 Draft (#26 overall)

The Report: It was an up and down year for Thompson, starting down before ending up. A hamate bone injury cost him time early in the season, while draining a lot of his offensive capabilities later in the season. Thompson got sent to the Arizona Fall League where he posted an .861 OPS in 16 games, looking closer to the highly-rated prospect he was coming into the 2019 season. That said, the road ahead for Thompson is long. At the plate, Thompson struggles with pitch recognition, and has yet to show the game power to make up for a hefty strikeout rate, as he's more of a line drive hitter at present.

When he does get on base, Thompson has good wheels that also serve him well in the outfield. He lacks the elite profile of fellow prospect Leody Taveras, but his work in the field is far from a liability. Thompson is entering his fourth year of organized baseball at just 21, so the door is still wide open. The concerning part is entering that fourth year without showing much refinement at the plate. Without that, Thompson's future will remain hazy even with all the potential in the world.

Variance: High. The lack of consistency in his approach limits the ceiling on Thompson. There is significant upside past the OFP if something clicks, but there is little evidence of that happening so far.

Ben Carsley's Fantasy Take: I'm not quite ready to give up yet. We viewed Thompson as a top-50 dynasty league prospect not too long ago, and while the reports about his trouble with pitch recognition are discouraging, I won't hold a hamate injury against him. He's definitely a high-risk prospect, but Thompson still has the speed, athleticism, and ability to make hard contact that I'm inclined to gamble on. I view this as a good time to buy low on Thompson, even if I acknowledge that the odds of him paying off for you seem lower than they did a year or two ago.

The Next Ten

11 **Tyler Phillips** RHP
Born: 10/27/97 Age: 22 Bats: R Throws: R Height: 6'5" Weight: 191
Origin: Round 16, 2015 Draft (#468 overall)

Phillips has an athletic build on a 6-foot-5 frame with broad shoulders, a high waist, and a strong lower half. He has a clean delivery with a loose whippy arm action from a high three-quarters arm slot.

He works with two fastballs, a four-seamer that sits 93-94 and a two-seamer at 90-93 with heavy sink and arm-side action. His primary secondary is a plus changeup with excellent arm speed, plus tumble, and some fade. Phillips also includes an average curveball with a slurvy shape that occasionally will flash above average. He has solid feel for both of his secondaries and can locate them fairly consistently. Phillips likes to lean heavily on his fastball mix and when he's able to command the zone he works in all four quadrants effectively before utilizing a tunnel to get whiffs on the changeup. He mixes in the breaking ball for a change of speed or to try and catch a hitter off balance, but his changeup is his primary out pitch. Phillips has excellent control of all three offerings, but his fastball command can come and go, leading to bursts of hard contact from the opposition. Without improving consistency there, he's going to have enough bad innings to limit his effectiveness as a starting pitcher, but if he irons that out he could slot himself into the back of a major league rotation.

12 Davis Wendzel 3B
Born: 05/23/97 Age: 23 Bats: R Throws: R Height: 6'0" Weight: 205
Origin: Round 1, 2019 Draft (#41 overall)

It was a bit of a surprise when the Rangers selected Wendzel in the comp round of 2019 draft. Wendzel's shorter, stocky build doesn't match the body type of traditional Rangers draft picks—who tend to look more like say, Bubba Thompson—but you could argue that their upside seeking has persisted here despite the feel of a "safe college bat" pick. Perhaps the Rangers are merely adjusting which upside traits they prioritize; here, approach, quickness, and coordination over a projectable frame and foot speed. Wendzel has coordination, plus bat speed, and a top-tier approach at the plate, but his swing is currently tooled to always make contact way out in front of his body. As a result there is a smaller window to create quality contact, and when he does it's almost always to the pull side. With adjustments to swing mechanics, Wendzel could better tap into his innate quality hit-tool markers while maintaining his raw power.

Defensively Wendzel has impressive hands, reactions, and instincts. He plays both third base and short, although his fringy foot speed and lateral range will likely limit him to a corner infield or outfield position. He flashes plus arm strength to complete the profile of a player who could step into any corner and be an asset defensively.

All in all, Wendzel paints the picture of a future four-corners bench player who has more upside than you'd expect from a late-first-round college bat, but has significant issues to iron out before he's there. If swing adjustments happen while his body and approach hold steady, there's a potential above-average regular here down the line.

13 David Garcia C
Born: 02/06/00 Age: 20 Bats: B Throws: R Height: 5'11" Weight: 170
Origin: International Free Agent, 2016

At the Texas Rangers Futures Camp held in Frisco, Garcia saw his stock rise more than any other player on the field. Coming in with a reputation as a small-bodied catcher with quality defensive markers, Garcia showed up with a reasonably mature build with good muscle both on his upper and lower halves. There's still room for more, but he's well on his way.

Garcia was even better than advertised defensively. His hands glided to receive the ball and strong wrists stopped it dead in its tracks after contact with the glove. He worked it well to all corners of the plate with natural movements. Footwork on blocks were second nature and he took a group of bad pitches in the dirt without one getting away from him. He popped 1.89 to second, showing a quick transfer and plus arm strength. The switch-hitter has above-average bat speed and quality hand-eye, portenting good contact abilities.

His pitch recognition wasn't nearly as raw as you'd expect for a hitter off the bus from short-season, and Garcia flashed gap-to-gap power, but his teenaged frame only produces below-average raw power, although that should bump up with further strength gains.

Garcia currently profiles as a tandem defense-first catcher with above-average regular upside if he can continue to add raw strength and get some power to transfer into games.

14 Anderson Tejeda SS
Born: 05/01/98   Age: 22   Bats: B   Throws: R   Height: 5'11"   Weight: 160
Origin: International Free Agent, 2014

Another victim of the evil curse placed upon Rangers infield prospects, Tejeda only played 43 games in Kinston before a subluxed shoulder ended his 2019. Tejeda is an enigmatic player who has yet to put it all together. His arm in the field is strong enough for shortstop and third base, he showed a power surge in 2018 with 18 bombs, and won't be 22 until next May. Not unlike a couple players on the list above him, Tejeda would do well to work on being more patient at the plate. Combining a more refined eye for what to lay off with his prowess for driving balls would vault him up the list in a system that has an assortment of shortstops below Double-A. The shoulder injury is worrisome, but indications are that Tejeda will make a full recovery in time for next season.

15 Jonathan Ornelas SS
Born: 05/26/00   Age: 20   Bats: R   Throws: R   Height: 6'1"   Weight: 178
Origin: Round 3, 2018 Draft (#91 overall)

Ornelas is definitely closer to 10 than 20 on this list and a strong candidate for a breakout next season. He didn't put up huge numbers this season, but held his own as a teenager in full-season ball and showed off a wide array of skills. Ornelas is an excellent defender, mainly at shortstop but he also showed well in stints at second and third. He's got the range, arm, and instincts for the six, and those tools play well at the other spots too. He's promising at the plate as well, with a quick bat, plus hands and strong wrists that consistently produce very hard contact. Mainly pull-oriented, Ornelas has shown the ability to adjust to and slice offspeed pitches the other way when necessary. Solid and wiry strong, the former third-rounder projects for a bit of power as he continues to acclimate himself to pro ball. Good utility types who can hit and play quality defense are always nice pieces to have.

16 Julio Pablo Martinez   OF
Born: 03/21/96   Age: 24   Bats: L   Throws: L   Height: 5'9"   Weight: 174
Origin: International Free Agent, 2018

The Cuban defector arrived to the Rangers system with a lot of hype. Some of that has been well-deserved; 15 homers between Low and High-A last season paired with borderline elite speed gave Martinez the base for a strong center field profile. The downside to that power was significant swing-and-miss issues as he struck out 156 times in 500 plate appearances. An aggressive approach paired with pitch recognition politely described as "has room to improve" keeps Martinez from reaching his full potential as a prospect. With year three of affiliated ball on deck, Martinez's ability to get on base more will be crucial to his development and advancement. There's a good chance Martinez will also see more games in the corner outfield positions in 2020, as it's likely that he'll share a roster with Rangers top prospect Leody Taveras for some of the season. A 24-year-old who hasn't cracked Double-A would be running out of prospect time normally, but Martinez's background makes it less of an issue here. Still 2020 is a big year for Martinez, who needs to take a step forward with the bat to maintain his prospect status.

17 Keithron Moss   IF
Born: 08/20/01   Age: 18   Bats: B   Throws: R   Height: 5'11"   Weight: 165
Origin: International Free Agent, 2017

Many years ago my father had a Lebanese roommate in Hartford or New Britain, I forget which. He had just gotten out of the service. I should remember, because I've heard this story many times. He always brings up the lamb tartare his roommate's mother made, and how it was one of the best dishes he ever had. Moss is rawer than that kibbeh nayyeh. There's the potential for a power over hit corner bat here. Not as tasty an outcome, but not too bad either.

18 Taylor Hearn   LHP
Born: 08/30/94   Age: 25   Bats: L   Throws: L   Height: 6'5"   Weight: 210
Origin: Round 5, 2015 Draft (#164 overall)

Murphy's Law hit the 25-year-old lefty hard this year. After four games for Triple-A Nashville, Hearn got called up for his major league debut against Seattle. Hearn threw a third of an inning, gave up five runs, and left with an elbow injury never to be seen again for the rest of 2019. Barring an unannounced setback, Hearn will be able to resume his career in 2020, and he was a top-flight pitching prospect before the mysterious elbow ailment. It's hard to know what we'll see from Hearn when he retakes the diamond, but pre-injury Hearn had a fastball around 93-94 with a good changeup and fringey breaking ball. After almost a full year on the shelf, however, it'll be good to see Hearn do anything involving throwing a baseball.

19 Ronny Henriquez   RHP
Born: 06/20/00   Age: 20   Bats: R   Throws: R   Height: 5'10"   Weight: 155
Origin: International Free Agent, 2017

Possessed of a fast arm on a small body, Henríquez is likely to strike many as a future reliever as he climbs the ladder and gains more exposure. It's an understandable assumption, as he really is short—listed at 5-foot-10 and not convincingly so—and to this point hasn't consistently made it deep into outings. It is far too early to give up on him as a starter, though, because he has a pair of interesting secondaries and he made strides with his command as a teenager in full-season ball. He has a plus fastball that holds velocity late into outings, sitting mid 90s and touching 97 with flashes of life up and sink down. His slider and split-change are both future above-average offerings, though he's not entirely consistent with either at present. He is a work in progress; his effectiveness will swing wildly from one start to the next, getting knocked around one week and looking dominant the next. But he's advanced for his age, and though he'll fly under-the-radar as far as right-handed pitching prospects in this organization are concerned, he's worth your attention.

20 Curtis Terry   1B
Born: 10/06/96   Age: 23   Bats: R   Throws: R   Height: 6'3"   Weight: 264
Origin: Round 13, 2015 Draft (#378 overall)

Guys like Curtis Terry don't often make top prospect lists in any form or fashion. A large man at 6-foot-3 and 246 pounds, he doesn't look the part of a baseball player in the modern era. He's—as the kids would say—thicc from his head to his toes. Yet, he does the thing you have to do: produce. Terry is a power hitter, swatting 25 home runs this year between two A-ball stops. The 2015 13th-round pick has blossomed into a fearsome bat, and earned his place on this list. You'll never see anything save for 1B or DH by his name on a lineup card, though his abilities at first base are underrated, but he hits and that's what teams care about these days. Terry has earned a chance to start 2020 at Double-A Frisco, and with no established starter at first base above him in the system Terry's ascent could take him further than anyone imagined.

Personal Cheeseball

PC **Kyle Cody   RHP**
Born: 08/09/94   Age: 25   Bats: R   Throws: R   Height: 6'7"   Weight: 245
Origin: Round 6, 2016 Draft (#189 overall)

We had Cody pegged for this spot even before he was surprisingly added to the 40-man, but given that nugget he might be the team's cheeseball too. He went unsigned as a 2015 Minnesota second-rounder out of Kentucky, and then was drafted the following year as a $150,000 sixth-round senior sign by Texas. The big Wisconsinite was one of our favorite rising pitching prospects in 2017, pairing a mid-90s fastball with plus sink and plane with a changeup and curveball that both flashed above-average to plus. It was a tantalizing arsenal, and he looked like he might move fast as a mid-rotation type…right up until his 2018 Tommy John surgery, which wiped out nearly all of his last two seasons. He's 25 with limited pro experience and none above A-ball, but it's a very interesting arm if he's healthy, and the Rangers thought enough of him to protect him from Rule 5. At the very least, he's a worthwhile 2020 follow.

Low Minors Sleeper

LMS **Pedro Gonzalez   OF**
Born: 10/27/97   Age: 22   Bats: R   Throws: R   Height: 6'5"   Weight: 190
Origin: International Free Agent, 2014

González has hovered near the back of prospect lists ever since he signed for a pretty hefty bonus a few years back, which he earned with qualities that jump out on first look. He's tall and lean, strong and athletic, with big raw power and a good arm. It is true that he has all of these virtues, and that they are just enough to keep him hanging around. He did have a solid age-21 season, making the Sally League All-Star Game in his second year at the level while pacing the circuit in homers. He covers all three outfield positions ably. Although he improved his approach a bit in his second pass at the league, he is still haunted by the demons that beset many a tools-driven prospect—swing-and-miss. And it is a lot of swing-and-miss. Long arms and difficulty picking up spin will do that, and it is hard to see these issues fading away when he faces higher levels of pitching. Still, who am I to bet against tools? He's worth stashing somewhere on this list just in case.

Top Talents 25 and Under (as of 4/1/2020)

1. Willie Calhoun
2. Leody Taveras
3. Josh Jung
4. Nick Solak
5. Joe Palumbo
6. Sam Huff
7. Hans Crouse
8. Nomar Mazara
9. Brock Burke
10. Sherten Apostel

Not unlike the Rangers themselves, the 25U list features potential ruling the day over the current reality. It's been the situation since the teardown of the major league team that began in 2017. The future is the focus, in the hope that it one day becomes a strong present.

Willie Calhoun tops the list in his final year of eligibility; the Yu Darvish trade's crown jewel overcame the warped meritocracy of modern baseball becoming a top half of the lineup hitter in the second half of the season. It was a victory for talent and resilience in the face of unnecessary obstacles.

It gets complicated behind him, but complicated in the delightful way of deciding between favorite dishes at a fabulous restaurant. The lower rankings of a major leaguer like Mazara likely raises eyebrows, but understand it's not without consideration. Mazara has plateaued as league-average, a major leaguer, yes, but one who doesn't stand out.

Taveras has an elite defensive profile, good enough to play in the majors right now. The ceiling is high on the 20-year-old conjuring All-Star dreams in the minds of fans and evaluators alike. Jung turns 22 soon, but has shown as more the 1b to Taveras' 1a after being taken in the top ten this past draft. On a team desperate for a franchise third baseman, Jung is a few steps away from seizing the position that Texas attempted to patch using a combination of Asdrubal Cabrera, Logan Forsythe, Isiah Kiner-Falefa, and Solak.

Huff, as noted above, is the high riser this season, riding a hot bat and competent behind the plate defense to becoming a top prospect. Catchers are odd and rare birds, with potential stars being worth their weight in gold. Huff occupies that status now for Texas, who is projected to run Jeff Mathis and Jose Trevino as a platoon for 2020.

Then there's the enigmatic gasoline-bringer Crouse. The 21-year-old has stuff for days, but durability concerns abound with the wiry righty. Those fears weren't alleviated with Crouse needing elbow surgery in October for bone spur removal. Crouse's ceiling is the sky, but don't look down because the floor might give you vertigo.

Mix in a major leaguer with injury concerns in Burke with young phenoms who had stellar 2019s in Apostel and Winn, and the Rangers' future is bright. With other names like Ronny Henriguez, Ricky Vanasco, Jonathan Ornelas, and many other baby Rangers bubbling under the surface this list is going to be one worth reading for the next half decade in the Lone Star State.

Part 3: Featured Articles

The Baseball Is Juiced (Again)

Robert Arthur

This article originally appeared at Baseball Prospectus on April 5, 2019.

It started when the normally reliable Chris Sale got lit up for three homers by the Mariners in the Red Sox's season opener. It was part of a record number of taters that flew on Opening Day, as starters from Sale to Zack Greinke were taken deep by the handful. Then Christian Yelich hit a home run in each of his first four games, tying yet another MLB record, this one for consecutive games with a dinger to start a season.

It didn't take long for fans and players to begin whispering and tweeting about the baseballs being juiced again. It's early yet for us to come to any definitive conclusion about the 2019 season, but preliminary data shows that the baseball has returned to its aerodynamic peak. Whether that means this season will smash home run records like 2017 did remains to be seen.

Before home run explosion over the last few years, no one worried too much about the baseball's air resistance. While MLB and Rawlings (the company that manufactures the official baseballs) kept track of dozens of metrics to make sure that the ball was consistent from month to month, they didn't measure drag.

But drag is incredibly important in determining how likely a hitter is to knock one out of the park. As baseballs become more aerodynamic, they travel further given a certain initial velocity. A deep fly ball that might have been caught at the warning track can instead go into the first row of the stands. A three percent change in drag coefficient can work to add about five feet to a well-hit fly ball, which can in turn increase home runs league wide by an astounding 10-15 percent.

It's possible to measure the aerodynamics of the baseball using the pitch-tracking radars currently in place in each MLB ballpark. By calculating the loss of speed from when the pitch is released to when it crosses the plate, you can directly measure the drag coefficient on the baseball. I first wrote about the role of decreasing drag in boosting home runs in 2017, and MLB's commission of scientists and statisticians later confirmed that the more aerodynamic baseballs

Texas Rangers 2020

in use that year were largely to blame for the spike in home runs. The same commission rejected some alternate hypotheses, like rising temperatures and a league-wide boost in launch angle pushing more balls over the fence.

The current era has featured some large fluctuations in drag coefficient, leading to first an explosion in 2016 and 2017, and then a dialing back of homers last year. Curious about the record-breaking home run tallies in the last few days, I used the same methodology to measure the aerodynamics of the baseballs so far in 2019.

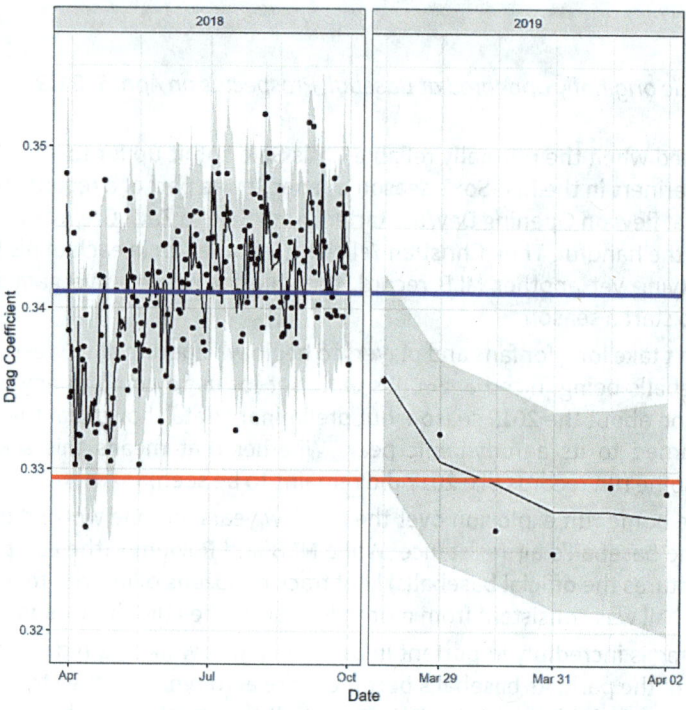

We're only a week into the 2019 season, but the drag numbers so far are among the lowest recorded in the last calendar year. With apologies for gory math, the current 2019 season average drag coefficient (the red line) would be below the 95 percent credible interval (the shaded area) for about nine-tenths of the 2018 season. (I used a Bayesian Random Walk model implemented in INLA to calculate these credible intervals, averaging the drag numbers in each game and adjusting for park.)

There were only a handful of six-day stretches in 2018 that had drag numbers below what we're seeing now, and most were in late June and early July. All of this means that 2019's data so far is quite a bit different than what we saw through most of last year.

136 - The Baseball Is Juiced (Again)

These drag coefficients factor out the effects of temperature and air density, so they aren't a product of April cold. However, the numbers could be deceptive if the radars used to track pitches have changed from year to year. I consulted with some experts within baseball who were not aware of any specific modifications to the radar this year that could produce this pattern, but it's an important caveat of which to be aware.

On the one hand, it's only been six days, and we don't quite have the statistical basis to say that these drag coefficients are unprecedented compared to 2018. On the other hand, we've witnessed about 5,000 fastballs so far this season, so it's not as if our sample size is small. At least so far, the baseball has played like it's much more aerodynamic than it was last year. In fact, the current drag coefficient is really only comparable to 2017, when the baseballs were more aerodynamic than they had been in at least a decade.

It's not just fancy radar tracking indicating that the baseball is flying through the air more easily. The current number of home runs per game (as of this writing) is the highest it's been since the heady days of 2017, the year that teams and players broke dinger-related records everywhere you looked. That's especially remarkable considering that we're in what is typically the coldest part of the regular season, when lower temperatures and higher winds tend to suppress offense and keep balls in the air within the park. Comparing only from April to April, this year's rate of home runs per fly ball is even a little bit higher than it was in 2017.

With that said, the current measurements are no guarantee that 2019 will be another year of record-shattering homer hitting. The trouble with the drag measurements is that they are not consistent from June to August, from week to week, or even sometimes from day to day. Whether because of natural manufacturing variation or differences in the underlying supplies of cowhide and thread that go into the baseballs, drag has a tendency to fluctuate up and down over the course of a year. So the homers that fly in the first week of April wouldn't necessarily clear the fence a week later.

It's possible that this one-week drop in drag coefficient subsides and the baseball returns to its 2018 levels. On the other hand, it's almost equally probable that the ball becomes even more slippery and flies ever farther. Either way, it's clear that the baseball's air resistance is something to keep an eye on for the remainder of the 2019 season.

—*Robert Arthur is an author of Baseball Prospectus.*

The Moral Hazard of Playing It Safe

Craig Goldstein

This article originally appeared at Baseball Prospectus on August 6, 2019.

A couple days prior to the trade deadline, amidst a sea of tranquility posing as the lead up to the trade deadline, Bob Nightengale took to Twitter. Nightengale, who was probably wearing his pants backwards at the time, tweeted that MLB GMs were coming around on the idea that the unified trade deadline should be moved back from July 31 to August 15, so they could better assess their positions in the standings and whether they should buy or sell. To which I said:

This might strike some as reductive and churlish. And it might be that, but it isn't really wrong, either. Jeff Quinton wrote a great piece discussing the environmental factors that enable front offices to avoid risk without upsetting the apple cart within their own fanbases. I don't believe that it goes far enough, however. His article gives us the proper framework through which to understand why these behaviors have been allowed to seep into front offices throughout the league. Understanding the reasons behind these actions are different from excusing them, though, and GMs should not be let off the hook for their non-competitive approach to the trade deadline (much less the offseason).

⚾ ⚾ ⚾

It's fair to say that fans as a group have rarely, if ever, been pro-player. It is also fair to say that in the time during and following the Moneyball revolution, the pendulum swung from fans who cared intensely about winning in the moment (and thus might be intolerant of a rebuilding approach) to fans who supported building a team that could compete throughout multiple seasons, viewing the playoffs as a crapshoot, with the thought that getting multiple bites at the apple was a better approach than taking a bigger bite in any one season.

There's nothing wrong with that approach, and I still find merit in that argument. However, it seems that the pendulum has swung too far in that direction. Teams are overvaluing some of the individual factors that make themselves long-term contenders rather than attempting to seize a championship when given the opportunity. It's a difficult needle to thread.

And surely, they (and those in similar positions) would have liked another two weeks to clarify where they stand so as to better marshal their resources. We've all asked for a few more minutes when staring at a menu. But all of these GMs and front office personnel are where they are to make difficult decisions. They have proprietary data and internal analysts dedicated to understanding their position relative to the rest of the league, and how any move in the here and now impacts their long-term vision. To complain (if that report is accurate) that over half the season is not enough to properly assess their season is bullshit of the highest order. Move the deadline, and you'd simply have increasingly discounted trade offers because teams would be acquiring even less control of anyone they're acquiring, rental or not.

Major league front offices are behaving like the managers they lampooned two decades ago. They're effectively sacrificing a runner to second in the ninth inning—not because it's the correct move, but rather because it is safe. It used to be that the phrase "moral hazard" was used to describe general managers who made ill-fated, short-sighted decisions aimed at locking in wins and securing their jobs at the expense of their team's future. Now, general managers are guilty of committing moral hazards in the opposite direction, playing it utterly safe and terrified of becoming scapegoats.

In lieu of bold action, they opt to pussyfoot around a current window of contention, choosing instead to play the long game and stack up years of control like they're blocks in a game of Jenga. GMs pass on signing quality players in free agency because the back-end of the deal might look bad, and because they might be able to squeeze out 70 percent of the production from a player who costs a tenth as much. That's a safer investment, too, because it's also hard to prove a negative—it's impossible to prove that Manny Machado would make the Mets a playoff team in 2019-2020, but it's easy to say that the back half of Robinson Cano's contract sucks. Owners, who rule over GM's jobs, are also humans with human brain processes that will always make the so-called albatross contract uglier than the road not taken.

These days, GMs are remembered for the bad deals they make and the surplus value they generate, not the acquisition of expensive, necessary talents that meet their market worth (or fall slightly short while still providing significant on-field value). And front offices know that one or two expensive misfires can cost them their jobs, no matter how many good deals they make.

No front office exemplifies this ethos more than the Toronto Blue Jays. General Manager Ross Atkins had this to say following the Blue Jays underwhelming trade deadline:

This is by no means the first time that an executive will cite years of control to justify their actions, which is often just another way of saying "don't look at what we got, look at how much we got of it." Atkins touts quantity to elide the discussion of quality—either, that of the players acquired, or those given up. Remember: the other teams presumably value years of control, too.

Atkins also had some thoughts to offer regarding free agents back in early 2018:

This ignores, of course, whether the player can create enough value in the front end of a contract to justify the longer term of a deal, and the decline that often occurs in the back end. It also ignores whether the player can fill a need the team requires and put them in a position to compete for and win a championship. But as teams seemingly avoid contention at all, where they might end up having to consider and later justify some of these tough decisions, we still see risk-averse approaches.

Anthony Fenech's article on two trades that recently extended GM Al Avila didn't make got at this issue rather well:

> Passing on those deals was defensible: Both players had yet to break out and trading [Michael] Fulmer—a pitcher who appeared to be a future ace, no matter his injury concerns—would have taken serious gumption, opening Avila up to strong criticism.

Avoiding strong criticism is something each of us can understand as a motivation, but the avoidance of criticism only matters if that criticism is valid. In Fulmer's case, shoving his injury concerns aside affects not only the years that the team controls him (he is currently missing a full season due to Tommy John surgery) but also the quality of those seasons, as his knee and elbow injuries combined to dampen his effectiveness even when healthy enough to pitch. But it was easy to present the then-current image of Fulmer as a top of the rotation pitcher who the team had under its domain for the next five seasons as something to build around. The status quo isn't nearly as often second-guessed as a decision that disrupts it.

⚾ ⚾ ⚾

MLB GMs are risk-averse to a fault. They are ivy-educated and consulting firm-approved, and yet they can't seem to avoid leaving wins on the table in their all-consuming lust for a non-existent $/WAR championship. They are supposed to zig when everyone else zags, and not merely pay lip service to the idea of zigging through a calculated PR plan built on convincing the fan base their approach is novel when it actually apes most of their competitors. Instead they've become far more concerned with making safe, accepted-by-the-new-common-wisdom decisions, such that our prior understanding of what a moral hazard is has become inverted.

I can't blame them entirely, and not only because of the reasons that Quinton illuminated in his article, but also because of the damage wrought by the introduction of the second wild card (WC2) spot. MLB's desire to have more teams in playoff contention has sparked anti-competitive behavior. Teams know now that they do not need to swing big as they assemble their roster because there is a good chance that a mediocre team can either catch fire and capture a division, or muddle along until they back into the WC2.

Simultaneously, the one-game playoff has neutered the WC1, putting an entire season on the flip of a coin like some sort of baseball-obsessed Anton Chigurh. While the one-game playoff makes sense as a way to increase the value of winning a division, it also means that if a front office doesn't like its chances of overcoming a behemoth like the Dodgers or Astros in the offseason, they have few incentives to chase glory. Similarly, the relative inaction in the NL Central at the trade deadline—despite a wide open division—can be explained by the idea that any high-variance investment could still result in only a wild card (or worse) result, given the mere two months left in the season to make an impact.

⚾ ⚾ ⚾

As stated at the top, we should not confuse reasons for excuses. The implementation of the second wild card is just one of many environmental factors that influence how each front office operates. I am convinced that it is one of the larger factors, but I am also convinced that organizations need to shed the yoke of "efficiency at all costs" so that they can instead pursue competition, as the spirit of the game intends. Until they do, we're all deadline losers.

—*Craig Goldstein is an author of Baseball Prospectus.*

Index of Names

Allard, Kolby	52	Gonzalez, Pedro	112, 129
Allen, Cody	54	Goody, Nick	66
Andrus, Elvis	20	Guerrieri, Taylor	114
Apostel, Sherten	94, 122	Guzmán, Ronald	34
Barlow, Joe	114	Hearn, Taylor	106, 127
Biddle, Jesse	114	Heineman, Scott	36
Bird, Greg	95	Henriquez, Ronny	114, 128
Bird, Kyle	56	Herget, Jimmy	107
Burke, Brock	58, 122	Hernandez, Jonathan	114
Calhoun, Willie	22	Huang, Wei-Chieh	114
Chavez, Jesse	60	Huff, Sam	96, 120
Chirinos, Robinson	24	Jung, Josh	97, 118
Choo, Shin-Soo	26	Jurado, Ariel	68
Cody, Kyle	104, 129	Kelley, Shawn	70
Crouse, Hans	105, 121	Kiner-Falefa, Isiah	38
Dillard, Tim	114	Kluber, Corey	72
Dowdy, Kyle	114	Law, Derek	74
Duffy, Matt	28	Leclerc, José	76
Evans, Demarcus	114	Lyles, Jordan	78
Farrell, Luke	114	Lynn, Lance	80
Federowicz, Tim	112	Martin, Brett	82
Flynn, Brian	114	Martinez, Julio Pablo	112, 127
Forsythe, Logan	112	Mathis, Jeff	40
Frazier, Todd	30	Méndez, Yohander	108
Gallo, Joey	32	Minor, Mike	84
Garcia, Adolis	112	Montero, Rafael	86
Garcia, David	125	Moss, Keithron	127
García, Luis	62	Nicasio, Juan	88
Gibaut, Ian	114	Odor, Rougned	42
Gibson, Kyle	64	Ornelas, Jonathan	126
Gomez, Jeanmar	114	Palumbo, Joe	90, 119

Phillips, Tyler 114, 124
Ragans, Cole 109
Sampson, Adrian 114
Santana, Danny 44
Seise, Chris 98
Solak, Nick 46, 119
Speas, Alex 110
Springs, Jeffrey 114
Swihart, Blake 112
Taveras, Leody 99, 117
Tejeda, Anderson 100, 126
Terry, Curtis 128
Thompson, Bubba 101, 124
Travis, Sam 48
Trevino, Jose 50
Vanasco, Ricky 111
Vólquez, Edinson 92
Walker, Steele 102
Wendzel, Davis 125
White, Eli 103
Winn, Cole 112, 123